POSITIVE AFFIRMATIONS

for

BLACK WOMEN

**Build Confidence and Self-Esteem
Attract Success, Wealth, Love
and Create the Life You Deserve**

SHANICE DANIELS

Dear Beautiful Soul,

Welcome to your journey of self-love, empowerment, and unapologetic authenticity. This book was created with you in mind—the woman who carries so much on her shoulders, who pours into others tirelessly but often forgets to pour into herself. If you've ever felt unseen, undervalued, or stretched too thin, I want you to know something right now: you are enough.

For far too long, society has demanded so much from Black women while offering so little in return. We're expected to be strong, resilient, and capable at all times. But what about you—your heart, your dreams, your well-being? What about your need to rest, to heal, and to feel deeply loved and appreciated for exactly who you are?

That's why this book exists. It's not just a collection of words; it's a tool, a friend, a reminder that you deserve the same love, care, and grace you so freely give to others. The affirmations you'll find here are not just empty phrases. They are powerful declarations designed to uplift you, to help you release the weight of self-doubt, and to remind you of your limitless potential.

How to Use This Book

You don't need to set aside hours each day to benefit from affirmations. Just a few minutes in the morning or before bed is enough to plant seeds of positivity and growth. Think of this book as your daily guide—a resource you can turn to when you need encouragement, inspiration, or simply a moment to breathe.

Here's how you can make the most of it:

1. **Start Small:** Pick one or two affirmations each day that resonate with you. Write them down, say them out loud, or repeat them silently during a quiet moment.
2. **Be Consistent:** Make affirmations part of your routine. Whether it's over your morning coffee, during your commute, or as part of your bedtime ritual, these small moments add up.
3. **Reflect:** Take time to notice how these affirmations make you feel. Keep a journal nearby to jot down any shifts in your mindset or emotions.
4. **Personalize It:** Feel free to tweak the affirmations or add your own. This is your journey—make it yours.

This Is About You

This book is divided into chapters that cover every area of your life—from building unshakable self-confidence to finding peace in the chaos, from fostering healthy relationships to creating a legacy you're proud of. Each chapter offers 150 affirmations designed to meet you where you are and guide you toward where you want to be.

These affirmations are more than just words. They're a way to reclaim your narrative, to stand in your truth, and to affirm to yourself and the world that your life, your voice, and your dreams matter.

A Journey of Transformation

I know life gets busy. You may be thinking, When will I have time for this? But let me tell you something: just as you find time to care for others, you can find time to care for yourself. Even five minutes a day can make a difference.

And if it feels awkward at first—that's okay. It's normal. Speaking affirmations into existence can feel foreign when you're used to silencing your own needs. But trust me, the more you say them, the more you'll believe them. And the more you believe them, the more you'll see their power transform your life.

So, take a deep breath. This is your time. You are not alone in this journey. Together, we'll embrace the beauty of who you are, affirm your greatness, and celebrate all the possibilities waiting for you.

Because you deserve nothing less.

PART 1:

UNDERSTANDING THE POWER OF AFFIRMATIONS

What Are Affirmations?

Before we dive into the affirmations themselves, let's take a moment to understand what they are and why they matter. Affirmations are simple yet powerful statements that help you challenge and overcome negative thoughts. They're not just words you say out loud—they're declarations of your truth, a way of reminding yourself who you are and what you deserve.

Think of affirmations as seeds. When you plant them and nurture them consistently, they grow into beliefs. Over time, these beliefs influence how you see yourself, how you move through the world, and how you respond to life's challenges.

For example, instead of waking up and letting that little voice in your head say, "I'm so tired; I'll never get everything done today," you can tell yourself, "I have all the energy and focus I need to accomplish what matters most." It might feel strange at first, but with practice, it becomes second nature.

Why Affirmations Are Essential for Black Women

Let's be real. As Black women, we face unique challenges every day—sometimes subtle, sometimes blatant, but always heavy. Whether it's navigating microaggressions at work, pushing past generational trauma, or fighting to be seen and valued in a society that often overlooks us, the world doesn't always make space for us to just be.

Affirmations are one way we can create that space for ourselves. They're not about ignoring the struggles we face but about building the resilience to rise above them. They're about reminding ourselves that we are worthy, capable, and powerful, even when the world tries to tell us otherwise.

When you speak affirmations, you're reclaiming your narrative. You're taking control of your inner dialogue and deciding what story you want to live out. And let's be clear: your story is not one of lack or limitation. Your story is one of strength, beauty, and infinite possibility.

THE SCIENCE BEHIND AFFIRMATIONS

If you're wondering, "Does saying these things out loud actually work?" the answer is yes—and there's science to back it up. Affirmations are rooted in the concept of neuroplasticity, which is the brain's ability to rewire itself based on repeated thoughts and behaviors.

Here's how it works:
- When you repeat positive affirmations, you're essentially training your brain to focus on the good instead of dwelling on the negative.
- Over time, this consistent practice strengthens the neural pathways associated with positive thinking and self-belief.
- The more you affirm yourself, the more natural it becomes to believe in your own worth and capabilities.

It's not magic; it's intention. When you combine affirmations with action, you create real, tangible change in your life.

Affirmations as a Tool for Transformation

Let me share something personal. For years, I struggled with negative self-talk. I'd look in the mirror and pick myself apart, or I'd compare myself to others and feel like I didn't measure up. But when I started practicing affirmations, something shifted. Slowly but surely, I began to see myself differently. I stopped being my own worst critic and started becoming my biggest cheerleader.

That's what I want for you, too.

Affirmations can be a powerful tool for:

- **Healing from past wounds** by replacing self-doubt with self-compassion.
- **Building confidence** by focusing on your strengths instead of your shortcomings.
- **Attracting opportunities** by aligning your thoughts with your goals.
- **Strengthening your resilience** so you can face challenges with grace and courage.

And here's the thing: this isn't about pretending everything is perfect. It's about equipping yourself with the mindset to navigate life's ups and downs without losing sight of your worth.

A Practice Rooted in Our Legacy

As Black women, affirmations are not new to us. They've always been part of our legacy, even if we didn't call them that. Think about the prayers your grandmother whispered over you, the hymns sung in church, or the mantras spoken during moments of struggle. These were all affirmations—words of faith, strength, and hope passed down through generations.

When you practice affirmations today, you're continuing that legacy. You're standing on the shoulders of those who came before you, honoring their resilience while creating a path for those who will come after you.

Start Where You Are

Maybe you've never tried affirmations before, or maybe you've tried and felt silly or skeptical about it. That's okay. This is a journey, not a sprint. The key is to start where you are and permit yourself to grow into this practice.

You don't have to be perfect at it. You just have to be willing.

As you move through this book, remember that every affirmation is an opportunity to affirm your truth, rewrite your story, and step into your power. You deserve this—and more. Let's get started.

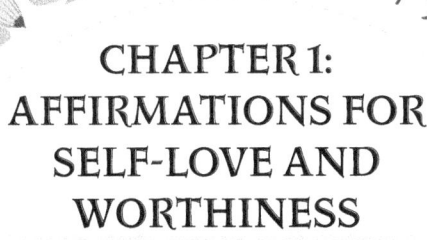

CHAPTER 1:
AFFIRMATIONS FOR
SELF-LOVE AND
WORTHINESS

"Your crown has been bought and paid for.
Put it on your head and wear it."
—Maya Angelou

Self-love isn't just a buzzword—it's your birthright. As Black women, we often hear messages about being "too much" or "not enough." We're told to shrink ourselves, to be humble, to put everyone else first. But here's the truth: you deserve to love yourself boldly, completely, and without apology.

Maya Angelou's words remind us that our worth isn't something we need to earn—it's already ours. We just need to claim it. This chapter is about remembering who you are and embracing every part of yourself, from your achievements to your struggles, from your confidence to your doubts.

Whether you're just starting your self-love journey or need a reminder of your worth, these affirmations are here to help you build an unshakeable foundation of self-love. They're not about becoming someone new—they're about embracing who you already are and nurturing the relationship you have with yourself.

150 Affirmations for Self-Love and Worthiness

1. I am enough, just as I am.

2. I am worthy of love, respect, and kindness.

3. My value is not determined by others' opinions of me.

4. I honor my journey and the progress I've made.

5. I release the need to prove my worth—I am already deserving.

6. My presence is a gift to the world.

7. I am proud of the woman I am becoming.

8. I choose to see myself through the eyes of love.

9. I am worthy of taking up space and having my voice heard.

10. I am complete and whole, just as I am.

11. I am deserving of all the good things life has to offer.

12. I am more than enough in every way.

13. I am not my mistakes; I am my possibilities.

14. I embrace my flaws as part of my unique beauty.

15. I am worthy simply because I exist.

16. I forgive myself for past mistakes and allow myself to grow.

17. I am gentle with myself because I deserve care and compassion.

18. I release the need for perfection and embrace my humanity.

19. I celebrate my progress, no matter how small.

20. I give myself permission to rest and recharge.

21. I am patient with myself as I learn and grow.

22. I choose to speak kindly to myself today.

23. My self-love inspires others to love themselves.

24. I honor my feelings and listen to what my heart needs.

25. I am worthy of prioritizing my well-being.

26. I let go of the harsh judgments I've placed on myself.

27. I deserve the same forgiveness I offer to others.

28. I am allowed to make mistakes and learn from them.

29. I choose to nurture myself with love and care.

30. My inner critic does not define me—I choose self-love.

31. I am beautiful, inside and out.

32. My scars tell a story of resilience and strength.

33. I celebrate my unique features and love the skin I'm in.

34. My body is a temple, and I treat it with care.

35. I am strong, capable, and confident.

36. My beauty radiates from within.

37. I love the way I show up for myself and others.

38. I am grateful for my body and all that it allows me to do.

39. My strength is a reflection of the challenges I've overcome.

40. I am proud to be a Black woman, and I honor my heritage.

41. I am a masterpiece in progress.

42. My beauty is defined by my authenticity and confidence.

43. I stand tall and embrace my uniqueness.

44. My natural beauty is radiant and undeniable.

45. I am worthy of feeling beautiful and confident every day.

46. I am deserving of happiness and joy.

47. I allow myself to celebrate my victories, big and small.

48. I create a life filled with love, peace, and fulfillment.

49. I release guilt and welcome joy into my life.

50. My happiness is my responsibility, and I embrace it fully.

51. I find joy in the simple moments of every day.

52. I am allowed to feel good about myself and my life.

53. My laughter is a reflection of my light within.

54. I am grateful for the joy that surrounds me.

55. I deserve to live a life that feels good to me.

56. I invite joy into my life every single day.

57. I find beauty and happiness in the little things.

58. My heart is open to all the joy the universe has to offer.

59. I celebrate the joy of being alive today.

60. I am worthy of experiencing true happiness.

61. I trust myself to make the right decisions for my life.

62. I am confident in my abilities and my potential.

63. I walk through life with purpose and determination.

64. I radiate confidence and self-assurance.

65. I am capable of achieving greatness.

66. My confidence grows stronger every day.

67. I believe in myself and my dreams.

68. I am proud of my accomplishments and my journey.

69. I carry myself with confidence and grace.

70. I have everything I need to succeed.

71. I am proud of how far I have come.

72. My achievements are a reflection of my hard work and dedication.

73. I celebrate every victory, no matter how small.

74. I am worthy of recognition for all that I've accomplished.

75. I honor the effort I put into everything I do.

76. My journey is unique, and I'm proud of my progress.

77. I give myself credit for navigating life's challenges with grace.

78. I deserve to feel proud of the person I've become.

79. I am successful in my own way, on my own terms.

80. I celebrate the lessons I've learned along the way.

81. I trust myself to make the best decisions for my life.

82. I am in tune with my intuition and follow it with confidence.

83. I trust my ability to handle whatever comes my way.

84. I am capable of solving problems and finding solutions.

85. I am wise, resourceful, and resilient.

86. My instincts guide me toward what is best for me.

87. I trust the timing of my life and the process of growth.

88. I am confident in my ability to take care of myself.

89. I am strong enough to face any obstacle.

90. I trust that everything I need is already within me.

91. My path is mine alone, and I honor it fully.

92. I release the need to compare myself to others.

93. I am exactly where I am meant to be.

94. My journey is unfolding perfectly, even if I can't see it yet.

95. I embrace the uniqueness of my story.

96. I celebrate my individuality and what makes me different.

97. I release the pressure to be anything other than myself.

98. I am free to grow and evolve at my own pace.

99. My life is a reflection of my authenticity.

100. I trust the journey I am on and the person I am becoming.

101. I treat myself with the same kindness I show to others.

102. I am worthy of the love I so freely give.

103. I choose to love myself unconditionally.

104. I am gentle with myself, especially on hard days.

105. I deserve compassion, even when I make mistakes.

106. I am learning to love every part of myself.

107. My imperfections make me beautifully human.

108. I honor my needs and take time to care for myself.

109. I am patient with myself as I heal and grow.

110. I permit myself to love myself fully.

111. I have the right to set boundaries that honor my well-being.

112. I deserve relationships that respect and uplift me.

113. I release guilt for putting myself first.

114. My boundaries are a reflection of my self-love.

115. I am not responsible for others' happiness—I am responsible for my own.

116. I have the strength to say no when something doesn't serve me.

117. I surround myself with people who value and respect me.

118. I am worthy of relationships that feel safe and supportive.

119. I protect my peace by choosing what aligns with my values.

120. I am in control of my time, energy, and emotions.

121. I am stronger than I realize.

122. Every challenge I face makes me more resilient.

123. I am capable of handling anything that comes my way.

124. My worth is not diminished by setbacks or failures.

125. I am proud of my ability to rise after every fall.

126. I grow stronger and more confident with each passing day.

127. I trust myself to overcome life's challenges.

128. I am resilient, resourceful, and powerful.

129. My struggles do not define me—they empower me.

130. I am unstoppable in my pursuit of growth and happiness.

131. I am grateful for who I am and who I am becoming.

132. I welcome joy into my life with open arms.

133. My heart is full of gratitude for all that I have.

134. I choose to focus on the positive in every situation.

135. I am surrounded by love, beauty, and abundance.

136. I find joy in the simple pleasures of life.

137. I am thankful for my journey and the lessons it has taught me.

138. I radiate gratitude and attract even more to be thankful for.

139. I celebrate the gift of being alive today.

140. I deserve all the happiness that life has to offer.

141. I am the author of my own story.

142. I have the power to create the life I desire.

143. I am in control of my thoughts, actions, and emotions.

144. I choose to live authentically and unapologetically.

145. I am capable of achieving greatness on my terms.

146. I am a force to be reckoned with.

147. I have the courage to step into my power fully.

148. My potential is limitless, and I embrace it completely.

149. I am proud of the woman I am becoming each day.

150. I am worthy, powerful, and unstoppable.

CHAPTER 2:
AFFIRMATIONS FOR INNER PEACE AND EMOTIONAL HEALING

"You may not control all the events that happen to you, but you can decide not to be reduced by them."
—Maya Angelou

Inner peace doesn't mean everything in your life is perfect. It doesn't mean the absence of struggle or hardship. Instead, it's the ability to find calm within yourself, even when the world around you feels chaotic. Emotional healing is the same—it's not about forgetting or erasing pain but learning to grow from it and letting it transform you in ways that strengthen your spirit.

Every day, you may encounter situations that test your patience, challenge your resolve, or trigger old wounds. It's in those moments that affirmations can serve as a lifeline. They help you reconnect with your center, remind you of your resilience, and guide you toward healing.

Maya Angelou's words remind us that while life's challenges are inevitable, how we respond to them is what shapes our journey. This chapter is about reclaiming that power—choosing to be whole, choosing to release pain, and choosing peace over the noise.

Let these affirmations become part of your daily practice. Speak them aloud, write them in your journal, or carry them in your thoughts. With each repetition, you are planting seeds of healing and creating a sanctuary of peace within yourself.

150 Affirmations for Inner Peace and Emotional Healing

1. I am at peace with my past and present.

2. I let go of what no longer serves me.

3. I allow myself to feel and process my emotions fully.

4. I choose calmness over chaos.

5. I release the weight of resentment and embrace forgiveness.

6. My mind is a safe space for peace and clarity.

7. I am worthy of emotional healing and inner peace.

8. I forgive myself for holding onto pain longer than I needed to.

9. I deserve to heal, no matter how long it takes.

10. I am gentle with myself as I navigate my healing journey.

11. Each day, I release a little more of what no longer serves me.

12. I honor my emotions without letting them control me.

13. I choose peace, even in moments of uncertainty.

14. I am strong enough to face and release my pain.

15. I welcome peace into my life with open arms.

16. My healing is my priority, and I embrace it fully.

17. I permit myself to let go of old wounds.

18. I am free from the chains of anger and regret.

19. I forgive others for my peace, not for their approval.

20. I trust the process of my healing, even when it feels slow.

21. I am learning to be patient with myself.

22. I allow myself to breathe through life's challenges.

23. I am proud of how far I have come in my journey.

24. I release negative thoughts and welcome positive energy.

25. I am a work in progress, and that's okay.

26. I trust my ability to handle whatever comes my way.

27. My past does not define me—I define myself.

28. I choose to focus on what brings me peace and happiness.

29. I am safe in my body, mind, and heart.

30. I am not my mistakes; I am my potential.

31. I forgive myself for not knowing then what I know now.

32. I release guilt and embrace self-compassion.

33. I honor my boundaries as an act of self-love.

34. I let go of fear and trust that everything will work out.

35. My heart is open to healing and love.

36. I deserve relationships that feel safe and supportive.

37. I allow myself to rest and recharge without guilt.

38. My peace is more important than my need to please others.

39. I choose to let go of pain and hold onto joy.

40. I am grateful for the lessons my challenges have taught me.

41. I am free to grow beyond my pain.

42. I am stronger than my struggles.

43. I allow myself to release tension and relax fully.

44. I am grounded in this moment and at peace.

45. I am not defined by the opinions of others.

46. I am learning to trust myself again.

47. I embrace the healing power of time.

48. My mind is calm, my heart is at ease, and my soul is free.

49. I give myself grace as I navigate difficult emotions.

50. I choose to respond to life's challenges with wisdom and patience.

51. I am in control of my peace, and I protect it fiercely.

52. I trust that healing is a journey, not a destination.

53. I am resilient and capable of overcoming any obstacle.

54. My peace is my responsibility, and I claim it fully.

55. I release the need to have all the answers.

56. I learn from the past grateful for the opportunity to reflect and improve.

57. I trust the wisdom that comes from stillness.

58. I permit myself to feel joy even as I heal.

59. My peace is non-negotiable.

60. I allow myself to start fresh each day.

61. I release shame and embrace self-love.

62. I let go of what I cannot control and focus on what I can.

63. I am worthy of a life free from emotional pain.

64. I honor the lessons my pain has taught me.

65. I release fear and welcome courage into my heart.

66. I am grateful for the opportunity to grow and evolve.

67. I trust my ability to find peace, even in difficult moments.

68. I allow myself to embrace calmness in all areas of my life.

69. My mind is clear, my heart is open, and my soul is at peace.

70. I release the need to hold onto anger.

71. I choose to forgive because I deserve peace.

72. I am healing every day, in every way.

73. I am surrounded by love and support as I heal.

74. I trust that everything is unfolding as it should.

75. I am at peace with who I am becoming.

76. I release negativity and embrace positivity.

77. I choose to see challenges as opportunities for growth.

78. I am grateful for the healing that is taking place in my life.

79. I am free to let go and move forward.

80. I allow myself to fully experience the present moment.

81. I release the weight of the past and step into my future with peace.

82. My peace is a gift I give to myself every day.

83. I am learning to love myself more with each passing moment.

84. I trust that healing is possible for me.

85. I am resilient, courageous, and at peace.

86. I allow myself to rest and recharge.

87. I honor my journey and all it has taught me.

88. My peace is my power, and I claim it fully.

89. I am in charge of my emotions and my reactions.

90. I let go of what no longer serves me and make room for what does.

91. I trust that I am exactly where I need to be.

92. I am open to receiving healing and peace.

93. I choose to focus on the good in my life.

94. I am proud of how far I have come.

95. I am healing, growing, and thriving every day.

96. I am grateful for the love and peace that surround me.

97. I let go of anxiety and welcome calmness into my life.

98. I release old wounds and make space for healing.

99. I trust the process of my life, even when it feels uncertain.

100. I am free to move forward with peace in my heart.

101. I embrace peace as my natural state of being.

102. I am worthy of feeling safe and secure in my own mind.

103. I release judgment and replace it with compassion.

104. I honor my emotions and allow them to flow freely.

105. I am at peace with my past and excited for my future.

106. I am resilient, and I rise above every challenge.

107. I release the weight of guilt and welcome forgiveness.

108. My peace is a priority, and I protect it fiercely.

109. I allow myself to heal at my own pace.

110. I trust that my heart knows how to heal itself.

111. I am open to love, joy, and inner peace.

112. I am learning to let go of what no longer serves me.

113. I release fear and embrace courage.

114. I allow myself to be fully present in each moment.

115. I trust the journey of my healing and growth.

116. I am worthy of living a peaceful and fulfilling life.

117. I release the need to control everything and trust the process.

118. I am grateful for the peace I create in my life.

119. I choose to be kind and gentle with myself.

120. My heart is open to healing and peace.

121. I forgive myself for holding onto pain.

122. I release negativity and embrace positivity.

123. I am proud of the progress I have made in my healing.

124. I allow myself to feel peace in every moment.

125. I am healing in ways I never thought possible.

126. I trust that peace is always within reach.

127. I let go of what no longer aligns with my highest good.

128. I am deserving of a calm and peaceful mind.

129. I am worthy of a life filled with love and serenity.

130. I trust myself to find peace, even in difficult times.

131. I let go of worry and welcome calmness into my heart.

132. I embrace peace as my birthright.

133. I am healing my mind, body, and soul.

134. I release the need to dwell on the past.

135. I am grateful for the opportunity to start fresh each day.

136. I am safe, I am loved, and I am at peace.

137. I let go of all that weighs me down.

138. I am proud of the person I am becoming.

139. I release the need for approval and find peace within myself.

140. I am free from the burden of anger and resentment.

141. I trust my inner wisdom to guide me toward peace.

142. I am worthy of healing and happiness.

143. I release tension and invite calmness into my life.

144. I am grateful for the progress I've made on my healing journey.

145. I am at peace with myself and my life.

146. I allow myself to feel peace, even in uncertain times.

147. I release fear and replace it with trust.

148. I am proud of my ability to find peace in any situation.

149. I am healing, one breath at a time.

150. I am at peace with who I am and where I am going.

REFLECTION PROMPT:

Which affirmation felt like it was written just for you? Write it down, repeat it throughout the day, and reflect on how it makes you feel.

Inner peace and emotional healing are not destinations—they are ongoing processes. Each affirmation you say is a step toward greater calm, clarity, and freedom. Let these words guide you, ground you, and remind you of your infinite capacity for peace.

Let's move forward together.

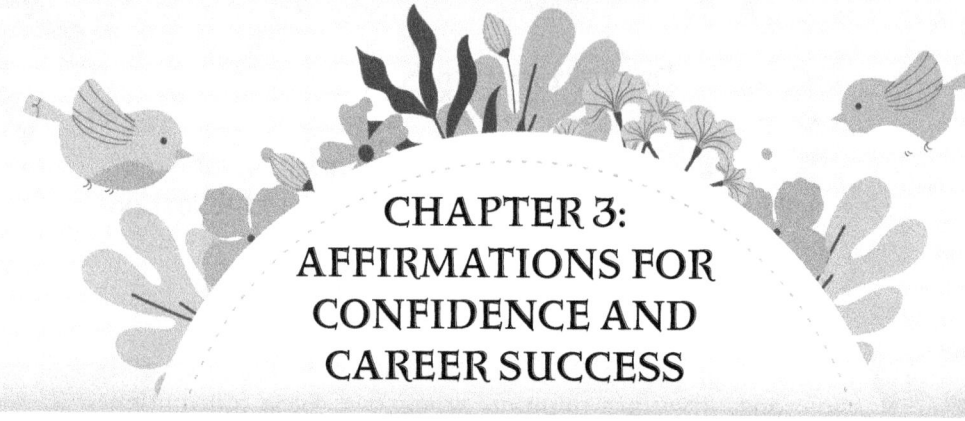

CHAPTER 3:
AFFIRMATIONS FOR
CONFIDENCE AND
CAREER SUCCESS

"If they don't give you a seat at the table, bring a folding chair."
—Shirley Chisholm

Confidence is the foundation of success. Whether you're pursuing a dream, navigating your career, or standing up for yourself, confidence allows you to show up fully and unapologetically. It's about knowing your worth, trusting your abilities, and believing in your power to create the life you want.

For many of us, confidence can feel like a battle. We've been told to shrink ourselves, not to aim too high, or to second-guess our abilities. Shirley Chisholm's words remind us to claim our space boldly—because if we don't, who will?

This chapter is about building unshakable confidence and aligning that confidence with your professional growth. The affirmations here are designed to help you embrace your strengths, speak your truth, and own your power in every aspect of your career. Let them remind you that your success is not just possible—it's inevitable when you trust in yourself.

150 Affirmations for Confidence and Career Success

1. I believe in my ability to achieve great things.

2. I am confident in my unique skills and talents.

3. I trust myself to make the best decisions for my career.

4. I have the courage to step outside my comfort zone.

5. My voice matters, and I use it with confidence.

6. I am worthy of every opportunity that comes my way.

7. I am a valuable asset in any workplace or team.

8. I approach challenges with curiosity and determination.

9. I deserve recognition for my hard work and dedication.

10. I embrace new opportunities with excitement and confidence.

11. I am capable of achieving my goals, no matter how big.

12. I am open to learning and growing every day.

13. My ideas are innovative and valuable.

14. I trust my instincts to guide me in the right direction.

15. I am fearless in the pursuit of my dreams.

16. I turn obstacles into opportunities for growth.

17. I bring a unique perspective to every situation.

18. I am confident in my ability to create success.

19. My potential is limitless, and I embrace it fully.

20. I am deserving of promotions, raises, and career advancements.

21. I am in control of my career and my future.

22. I am a leader, and I inspire others with my confidence.

23. My confidence grows stronger with every success I achieve.

24. I am resilient and can overcome any professional setback.

25. I show up authentically in every space I enter.

26. I trust my ability to handle difficult conversations with grace.

27. I am worthy of pursuing a career I love.

28. I take pride in the work I do and the value I bring.

29. I am not afraid to advocate for myself and my needs.

30. I am confident in my ability to learn new skills quickly.

31. I celebrate my achievements and use them as stepping stones.

32. I am capable of managing my time and energy effectively.

33. I am deserving of a career that aligns with my passions.

34. My confidence inspires those around me to believe in themselves.

35. I am not afraid to ask for what I want.

36. I attract opportunities that align with my highest potential.

37. I am constantly growing and evolving in my career.

38. I am proud of the professional I am becoming.

39. I take bold steps toward the career I desire.

40. I create opportunities for myself by showing up fully.

41. My hard work and dedication always pay off.

42. I am not afraid to take risks in the name of growth.

43. I trust the process of my professional journey.

44. I am confident in my ability to lead and inspire others.

45. I deserve to be in spaces where my talents are celebrated.

46. I am not afraid to fail because failure is part of growth.

47. I am worthy of respect and appreciation in my career.

48. I create success through focus, determination, and passion.

49. I take responsibility for my career and my choices.

50. I am not afraid to take up space and be heard.

51. I embrace feedback as a tool for growth and improvement.

52. I am constantly learning and expanding my skill set.

53. I have the courage to create the career of my dreams.

54. My confidence opens doors to incredible opportunities.

55. I approach every challenge as a chance to grow stronger.

56. I am worthy of recognition for my unique contributions.

57. I trust that my career is unfolding exactly as it should.

58. I am confident in my ability to network and build connections.

59. I am fearless in pursuing what sets my soul on fire.

60. I am in charge of my career, and I steer it with confidence.

61. My confidence grows with every step I take toward my goals.

62. I am a problem-solver and find creative solutions with ease.

63. I am not afraid to negotiate for what I deserve.

64. I am proud of the progress I've made in my career journey.

65. I am open to new opportunities that align with my passions.

66. My career is a reflection of my unique talents and vision.

67. I trust that every step I take leads me closer to my goals.

68. I am confident in my ability to lead by example.

69. I am grateful for the opportunities I've been given and those yet to come.

70. I am deserving of a career that challenges and fulfills me.

71. I am not afraid to make bold decisions that align with my values.

72. I celebrate the courage it takes to pursue my dreams.

73. I am a magnet for success and abundance in my career.

74. I have the power to create a career that brings me joy and fulfillment.

75. My confidence shines in every interaction and opportunity.

76. I am not afraid to start over if it means building the career I want.

77. I am deserving of mentorship and guidance as I grow.

78. I am fearless in asking for what I need to succeed.

79. I am worthy of respect, recognition, and success.

80. I bring value to every role and project I take on.

81. I approach every challenge with confidence and determination.

82. My confidence is unshakable, even in the face of uncertainty.

83. I am proud of the work I do and the impact I make.

84. I am deserving of a career that reflects my passions and values.

85. I am not afraid to step into leadership roles.

86. I trust my ability to navigate professional challenges with grace.

87. I am a trailblazer, creating new paths for others to follow.

88. My confidence attracts success, opportunity, and abundance.

89. I am capable of balancing ambition with self-care.

90. I celebrate every milestone in my professional journey.

91. I am worthy of pursuing a career that excites and fulfills me.

92. I am confident in my ability to meet and exceed expectations.

93. My work ethic and confidence set me apart from the rest.

94. I embrace opportunities to showcase my unique strengths.

95. I am proud of my ability to overcome challenges in my career.

96. I trust myself to make decisions that align with my goals.

97. I am confident in my ability to pivot when needed.

98. I am grateful for the courage it takes to show up every day.

99. I am fearless in owning my accomplishments.

100. I am ready for the next chapter of my professional journey.

101. I create success by showing up authentically and confidently.

102. I am worthy of building a career that aligns with my dreams.

103. My confidence inspires others to believe in themselves.

104. I am resilient and handle setbacks with grace.

105. I deserve to be in rooms where decisions are made.

106. I am fearless in claiming what is mine.

107. My confidence grows as I celebrate my wins.

108. I trust that my career path is uniquely mine.

109. I am capable of achieving the impossible.

110. My potential is limitless, and I embrace it every day.

111. I attract opportunities that align with my strengths and passions.

112. I am confident in the direction my career is heading.

113. I am bold in pursuing what sets my soul on fire.

114. I approach every opportunity with an open mind and heart.

115. I am deserving of success, abundance, and joy in my career.

116. I am confident in my ability to bring my vision to life.

117. My success is inevitable because I believe in myself.

118. I am proud of the journey I've taken to get where I am.

119. I embrace every opportunity to showcase my brilliance.

120. I am a force to be reckoned with in my career.

121. My confidence makes me unstoppable.

122. I am not afraid to dream big and take bold steps.

123. I am grateful for the courage to pursue my passion.

124. I am ready to seize every opportunity that comes my way.

125. I trust my ability to navigate challenges with ease.

126. I am a magnet for career success and fulfillment.

127. My confidence grows with every step I take toward my goals.

128. I am not afraid to ask for what I deserve.

129. I trust that my hard work and dedication will pay off.

130. I am confident in my ability to handle success with grace.

131. I am a leader, and I inspire others to reach their potential.

132. I am deserving of a career that excites and fulfills me.

133. I am not afraid to step outside my comfort zone.

134. I celebrate every victory, big or small, along my journey.

135. I am ready to take the next step toward my career goals.

136. I am confident in my ability to create a meaningful career.

137. I am bold, brave, and unstoppable in my pursuit of success.

138. I trust the process of building a career I love.

139. I am proud of the work I do and the difference I make.

140. I am confident in my ability to leave a legacy.

141. I approach every opportunity with confidence and excitement.

142. I am worthy of recognition and success.

143. I am fearless in owning my accomplishments.

144. My confidence sets me apart and makes me shine.

145. I am capable of achieving anything I set my mind to.

146. I am not afraid to challenge the status quo and innovate.

147. I am proud of the progress I've made in my career journey.

148. I am ready to embrace every opportunity for growth.

149. I trust that my skills and talents will open doors for me.

150. I am unstoppable when I believe in myself.

Reflection Prompt:

>>

Which affirmation speaks to where you are right now in your career? Write it down and use it as a mantra throughout your day. Reflect on how it makes you feel and what actions it inspires.

Confidence and career success are deeply connected. The more you believe in yourself, the more opportunities you'll create and embrace. Let these affirmations remind you of your power and push you to take bold, confident steps toward the life you deserve.

Now, let's keep building. Onward to the next chapter!

CHAPTER 4:
AFFIRMATIONS FOR HEALTHY AND FULFILLING RELATIONSHIPS

"Surround yourself with only people who are going to lift you higher."
—Oprah Winfrey

Relationships are one of the most beautiful yet complex aspects of life. Whether they're with family, friends, or romantic partners, healthy relationships require mutual respect, trust, and communication. They are where we grow, where we're challenged, and where we find comfort.

However, for relationships to flourish, they must start with one critical ingredient: self-worth. When you see your own value, you're better able to communicate your needs, set boundaries, and attract relationships that are uplifting and supportive. Oprah Winfrey's words remind us of the importance of being seen and heard—both by others and by ourselves and surrounding ourselves with supportive, encouraging, positive people.

This chapter is here to help you nurture healthier, more fulfilling connections. Whether you're looking to strengthen an existing relationship, release a toxic one, or simply cultivate more love in your life, these affirmations are designed to guide you toward deeper connection and mutual respect.

150 Affirmations for Healthy and Fulfilling Relationships

1. I deserve relationships that are rooted in love and respect.

2. I communicate my needs clearly and confidently.

3. I attract people who uplift and inspire me.

4. My relationships are safe spaces where I can be myself.

5. I am worthy of love, care, and support.

6. I surround myself with people who value and appreciate me.

7. I set boundaries that honor my well-being and peace.

8. I release toxic relationships to make space for healthier connections.

9. I am not afraid to ask for what I need in a relationship.

10. I trust myself to choose relationships that align with my values.

11. I deserve to be treated with kindness and respect in every relationship.

12. I am a loving and supportive partner, friend, and family member.

13. My love is powerful, and it attracts the right people into my life.

14. I choose relationships that help me grow and thrive.

15. I allow myself to be open and vulnerable with those I trust.

16. I deserve relationships that feel balanced and fulfilling.

17. I honor my boundaries as an act of self-respect.

18. I am patient and understanding in my relationships.

19. I release resentment and choose forgiveness for my peace.

20. My relationships are built on trust, honesty, and mutual respect.

21. I deserve to feel safe and secure in every connection.

22. I attract people who appreciate me for who I truly am.

23. I create relationships that are supportive and loving.

24. I communicate with love and compassion.

25. I am worthy of a relationship that feels aligned and healthy.

26. I show up authentically in all of my relationships.

27. I attract relationships that bring out the best in me.

28. I deserve relationships that feel peaceful and joyful.

29. I trust the process of building meaningful connections.

30. I release the fear of abandonment and embrace love with confidence.

31. I am deserving of friendships that are nurturing and kind.

32. My relationships reflect the love I have for myself.

33. I release the need to please others at the expense of my peace.

34. I am capable of resolving conflicts with patience and understanding.

35. I allow myself to receive love fully and without hesitation.

36. I am worthy of being loved deeply and authentically.

37. I trust my instincts when it comes to relationships.

38. I attract people who respect my boundaries and honor my time.

39. I deserve to feel appreciated in all of my relationships.

40. I let go of relationships that no longer serve my highest good.

41. I choose relationships that align with my values and goals.

42. I am proud of the way I show up for the people I care about.

43. My relationships are a source of joy and inspiration.

44. I trust the flow of love in my life.

45. I give and receive love freely and openly.

46. I attract people who celebrate my growth and achievements.

47. I am not afraid to be vulnerable with those who earn my trust.

48. My relationships are built on mutual respect and honesty.

49. I choose to see the best in the people I care about.

50. I let go of grudges and embrace forgiveness for my peace.

51. I am open to giving and receiving unconditional love.

52. My relationships are a reflection of my self-worth.

53. I am confident in my ability to create healthy connections.

54. I attract relationships that feel easy, aligned, and fulfilling.

55. I release relationships that drain my energy or dim my light.

56. I am deserving of love that feels safe and secure.

57. My relationships are built on trust and mutual understanding.

58. I communicate with honesty and compassion.

59. I attract people who respect my time, energy, and boundaries.

60. I am grateful for the love and support in my life.

61. I am a magnet for relationships that feel aligned and joyful.

62. I choose to focus on the positive aspects of my relationships.

63. I am worthy of friendships that are uplifting and empowering.

64. I release fear and embrace love with an open heart.

65. I trust the people in my life to show up authentically.

66. I attract relationships that feel nourishing and supportive.

67. My relationships grow stronger with open and honest communication.

68. I choose to approach conflicts with patience and grace.

69. I am worthy of being celebrated and loved unconditionally.

70. I honor the unique dynamics of each of my relationships.

71. I attract people who bring joy and laughter into my life.

72. I release relationships that no longer serve my highest good.

73. I am grateful for the deep connections I have with others.

74. I create relationships that are built on mutual trust and respect.

75. I attract partners and friends who are kind, loving, and supportive.

76. I am open to the love and connection the universe has for me.

77. I release jealousy and comparison in my relationships.

78. I trust the process of building meaningful connections.

79. I allow myself to be fully seen and heard in my relationships.

80. I am not afraid to advocate for my needs in every connection.

81. I am proud of the love I give and the love I receive.

82. I create space for healthy, balanced relationships in my life.

83. I am confident in my ability to nurture meaningful connections.

84. I choose relationships that feel aligned with my highest self.

85. I let go of fear and embrace love in all its forms.

86. My relationships are built on kindness and mutual respect.

87. I attract people who value and celebrate my uniqueness.

88. I deserve relationships that feel easy and joyful.

89. I am open to growing and evolving within my relationships.

90. I release toxic patterns and embrace healthy communication.

91. My relationships are a source of love, joy, and growth.

92. I allow myself to receive the love I deserve.

93. I choose to let go of resentment and make space for healing.

94. I am worthy of relationships that feel supportive and uplifting.

95. I trust myself to build connections that align with my values.

96. I approach my relationships with compassion and understanding.

97. I deserve relationships that inspire and empower me.

98. I am proud of the way I nurture the people I care about.

99. I choose to build relationships that reflect my highest self.

100. I am open to the love and connection the universe has for me.

101. I release fear and embrace love with an open heart.

102. I trust that the right people are coming into my life at the right time.

103. I am worthy of relationships that feel aligned and joyful.

104. I am grateful for the love and support in my life.

105. I communicate my needs clearly and confidently in every relationship.

106. I attract people who celebrate my growth and achievements.

107. I deserve to be surrounded by love and positivity.

108. I am open to giving and receiving unconditional love.

109. My relationships are a reflection of the love I have for myself.

110. I release the need to hold onto unhealthy connections.

111. I create relationships that inspire and empower me.

112. I am proud of the way I show up in my relationships.

113. I choose to focus on the positive aspects of my connections.

114. I deserve relationships that feel supportive and balanced.

115. I am not afraid to be vulnerable in healthy relationships.

116. I release toxic relationships to make space for love and light.

117. I honor my boundaries as a form of self-care.

118. I attract people who align with my values and energy.

119. I trust myself to navigate my relationships with wisdom.

120. My relationships are a source of love, trust, and growth.

121. I deserve relationships that feel nourishing and uplifting.

122. I am open to love and connection in all its forms.

123. I approach conflicts with patience and understanding.

124. I attract friendships that are genuine and empowering.

125. I trust the people in my life to respect and support me.

126. I release the need to control others and trust the flow of love.

127. My relationships are built on mutual respect and understanding.

128. I am confident in my ability to build healthy connections.

129. I allow myself to receive the love I deserve.

130. I choose relationships that bring peace and joy into my life.

131. I am grateful for the opportunity to connect deeply with others.

132. I release fear and open my heart to love.

133. I trust the process of building meaningful relationships.

134. I attract relationships that feel safe and supportive.

135. I am proud of the love I give and the love I receive.

136. I am confident in my ability to nurture meaningful connections.

137. I choose relationships that reflect my highest self.

138. I let go of jealousy and comparison in my relationships.

139. I create space for relationships that inspire and uplift me.

140. My relationships are a reflection of my inner peace and joy.

141. I am worthy of friendships that are kind and supportive.

142. I approach my relationships with love and authenticity.

143. I attract people who value and celebrate my uniqueness.

144. I trust that the right relationships are unfolding for me.

145. I am grateful for the deep connections I have in my life.

146. I deserve relationships that align with my values and dreams.

147. I trust my instincts to guide me in my connections.

148. I am open to the love and connection that life has to offer.

149. I approach every relationship with an open heart.

150. My relationships are a reflection of the love and respect I have for myself.

REFLECTION PROMPT:

Think about one relationship in your life that you'd like to nurture or improve. Which affirmation feels most relevant to that connection? How can you take a small step toward strengthening that relationship today?

Healthy relationships begin with the relationship you have with yourself. As you speak these affirmations, let them guide you toward connections that bring you peace, joy, and fulfillment. You deserve nothing less.

Let's continue building this foundation together. Onward to the next chapter!

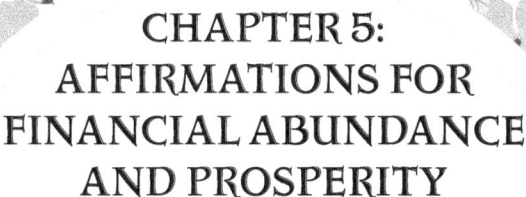

CHAPTER 5:
AFFIRMATIONS FOR
FINANCIAL ABUNDANCE
AND PROSPERITY

"I had to make my own living and my own opportunity. But I made it! Don't sit down and wait for the opportunities to come. Get up and make them."
—Madam C.J. Walker

Financial abundance isn't just about having money; it's about feeling secure, empowered, and in control of your financial future. It's about knowing that you deserve prosperity and that your hard work, creativity, and determination can create opportunities for wealth.

Madam C.J. Walker's words are a reminder that financial success starts with belief in your own abilities and the willingness to take bold steps. This chapter is here to help you embrace a mindset of abundance, overcome limiting beliefs about money, and create a life where financial freedom is not just a dream but a reality.

Whether you're working to increase your income, manage your finances wisely, or simply cultivate a healthier relationship with money, these affirmations are designed to guide you toward greater prosperity and peace of mind.

150 AFFIRMATIONS FOR FINANCIAL ABUNDANCE AND PROSPERITY

1. I am worthy of financial abundance and security.

2. I attract wealth and opportunities with ease.

3. Money flows to me in expected and unexpected ways.

4. I am capable of managing my money wisely and responsibly.

5. My financial goals are achievable, and I am making progress every day.

6. I am open to new opportunities for financial growth.

7. I release any fear or doubt I have about money.

8. I deserve to live a life of financial freedom and abundance.

9. I am confident in my ability to create wealth.

10. I attract opportunities that align with my financial goals.

11. My hard work and dedication create financial success.

12. I trust my ability to make smart financial decisions.

13. I am open to receiving abundance in all forms.

14. My wealth is a reflection of the value I bring to the world.

15. I release limiting beliefs about money and embrace abundance.

16. I am grateful for the financial blessings in my life.

17. I am a magnet for prosperity and success.

18. I manage my money with clarity and purpose.

19. I attract financial opportunities that align with my values.

20. I am capable of creating multiple streams of income.

21. My financial future is bright and secure.

22. I am confident in my ability to attract and maintain wealth.

23. I release any guilt I feel about wanting financial success.

24. I am worthy of receiving financial blessings.

25. I am in control of my financial destiny.

26. I am open to learning new ways to grow my wealth.

27. I attract clients, customers, and opportunities with ease.

28. I am confident in my ability to build generational wealth.

29. I choose to see money as a tool for good.

30. My income is constantly increasing.

31. I deserve to be well-compensated for my skills and talents.

32. I am financially free, and I enjoy the freedom that comes with it.

33. I am grateful for every dollar that flows into my life.

34. I am open to receiving financial gifts and surprises.

35. I trust that the universe is bringing me financial prosperity.

36. I am capable of achieving all of my financial goals.

37. My financial situation is improving every day.

38. I attract financial stability and success effortlessly.

39. I am deserving of all the wealth and abundance life has to offer.

40. I am in alignment with the energy of abundance.

41. I release any negative thoughts about money.

42. I attract abundance by being my authentic self.

43. I am proud of the financial progress I am making.

44. I am creating a life of wealth and prosperity.

45. I am not afraid to dream big when it comes to my finances.

46. I am grateful for the opportunities to grow my income.

47. I am confident in my ability to save and invest wisely.

48. I attract financial blessings because I believe I am worthy of them.

49. I am open to receiving financial advice and guidance.

50. I deserve to live a life free from financial stress.

51. I am building a solid financial foundation for myself and my family.

52. I release the fear of not having enough.

53. I am grateful for the money that flows into my life.

54. I am capable of creating a life of financial independence.

55. I attract abundance by being grateful for what I already have.

56. I am worthy of financial success and stability.

57. I am open to exploring new ways to increase my income.

58. I trust my ability to handle wealth responsibly.

59. I am confident in my ability to create a budget that works for me.

60. I attract financial abundance through my skills and creativity.

61. I deserve to live a life of comfort and security.

62. I am proud of my ability to build wealth and abundance.

63. I am not afraid to take risks to achieve my financial goals.

64. I am grateful for the financial lessons I have learned.

65. I am creating a legacy of wealth for future generations.

66. I trust the process of growing my financial wealth.

67. I am a magnet for financial success and abundance.

68. I attract opportunities that lead to financial growth.

69. I am open to receiving all forms of financial prosperity.

70. I am in control of my financial choices and decisions.

71. I am grateful for the freedom that financial abundance brings.

72. I attract wealth by aligning with my purpose.

73. I am confident in my ability to negotiate for what I deserve.

74. I release any fear of success and embrace abundance.

75. I am building a life of financial security and freedom.

76. I am proud of the financial decisions I make every day.

77. I trust that my financial needs will always be met.

78. I am capable of achieving financial independence.

79. I am grateful for the abundance that surrounds me.

80. I attract financial opportunities that bring me joy and fulfillment.

81. I am confident in my ability to handle financial challenges.

82. I am open to new ideas for creating wealth.

83. I attract abundance because I believe in my worth.

84. I am not afraid to ask for what I deserve financially.

85. I am creating a financial future that excites me.

86. I trust myself to make wise financial choices.

87. I attract financial stability through hard work and determination.

88. I am grateful for every financial opportunity that comes my way.

89. I am capable of achieving all of my financial dreams.

90. I attract wealth by being true to myself.

91. I am proud of the progress I've made in my financial journey.

92. I am deserving of a life filled with financial abundance.

93. I trust that I am on the right path to financial freedom.

94. I attract financial opportunities that align with my goals.

95. I am confident in my ability to manage and grow my wealth.

96. I release any doubts I have about my financial success.

97. I am open to receiving financial blessings every day.

98. I am grateful for the financial freedom I am creating.

99. I am proud of the financial independence I am building.

100. I attract wealth and abundance effortlessly.

101. I trust that the universe is working in my favor.

102. I am deserving of all the financial abundance life has to offer.

103. I am open to learning and growing in my financial journey.

104. I attract financial opportunities that align with my values.

105. I am confident in my ability to achieve financial security.

106. I release the fear of financial instability.

107. I am capable of creating a life of financial success.

108. I am grateful for every financial blessing in my life.

109. I am proud of the financial steps I take each day.

110. I trust that abundance is flowing to me now.

111. I am worthy of financial freedom and independence.

112. I attract wealth through my hard work and determination.

113. I release any doubts about my ability to create wealth.

114. I am open to exploring new ways to increase my income.

115. I am confident in my ability to achieve my financial goals.

116. I attract financial opportunities with ease and gratitude.

117. I trust the process of creating financial security.

118. I am proud of the financial progress I have made.

119. I release the fear of not having enough and embrace abundance.

120. I am grateful for the financial freedom I am building.

121. I am open to new opportunities for financial success.

122. I attract wealth by aligning with my purpose and passion.

123. I trust my ability to make wise financial decisions.

124. I am deserving of a life filled with financial security.

125. I am confident in my ability to manage my money wisely.

126. I attract financial opportunities that align with my values.

127. I am open to receiving abundance in all forms.

128. I am proud of my ability to create wealth and prosperity.

129. I trust that my financial needs will always be met.

130. I release fear and embrace financial freedom.

131. I am grateful for the abundance that flows into my life.

132. I attract financial blessings effortlessly and continuously.

133. I am confident in my ability to grow my wealth.

134. I am open to learning new ways to achieve financial success.

135. I attract financial stability through my hard work and dedication.

136. I am proud of the financial independence I am building.

137. I release any limiting beliefs about money and embrace abundance.

138. I trust my ability to create a secure financial future.

139. I am capable of achieving all of my financial dreams.

140. I attract wealth and prosperity with confidence.

141. I am grateful for every financial opportunity in my life.

142. I am open to receiving financial abundance every day.

143. I am proud of my ability to create financial security.

144. I trust that I am on the path to financial freedom.

145. I attract wealth and abundance effortlessly and continuously.

146. I am grateful for the financial blessings in my life.

147. I am confident in my ability to manage my finances wisely.

148. I am open to exploring new opportunities for financial growth.

149. I attract financial abundance through my creativity and passion.

150. I am proud of the financial future I am creating.

REFLECTION PROMPT:

Think about one financial goal you have. Which affirmation aligns most closely with that goal? Write it down and repeat it daily to stay focused on achieving it.

Financial abundance begins with your mindset. These affirmations are here to remind you of your worth, your potential, and your power to create the financial future you deserve. Let's keep building on this foundation. Onward to the next chapter!

CHAPTER 6:
AFFIRMATIONS FOR
HEALTH, WELLNESS,
AND SELF-CARE

"Many of us, we have a hard time putting ourselves on our own priority list, let alone at the top of it ...And that's what happens when it comes to our health as women. We are so busy giving and doing for others that we almost feel guilty to take that time for ourselves."
—Michelle Obama

Health is more than just the absence of illness—it's about feeling strong, balanced, and vibrant in every aspect of your life. It's about caring for your body, mind, and spirit with the same love and attention you give to everything else in your life.

Michelle Obama's wisdom reminds us of the importance of self-care and wellness. We often focus on taking care of others or achieving our goals, but without a foundation of good health, everything else becomes harder to sustain. Prioritizing wellness isn't selfish; it's essential.

This chapter focuses on affirmations that will encourage you to nurture your body, embrace rest, and prioritize your overall well-being. These affirmations will inspire you to cultivate healthy habits, honor your body's needs, and create a life rooted in balance and care.

150 Affirmations for
Health, Wellness, and Self-Care

1. I honor my body and treat it with care and respect.

2. I deserve to feel healthy, strong, and vibrant.

3. I nourish my body with wholesome foods and positive energy.

4. I am grateful for the health and vitality I experience every day.

5. I prioritize my well-being and listen to my body's needs.

6. I create space in my life for rest and relaxation.

7. My body is my home, and I cherish it.

8. I am strong, capable, and full of energy.

9. I permit myself to rest when I need it.

10. I am worthy of taking time for self-care.

11. I make choices that align with my health and happiness.

12. My body knows how to heal, and I trust its wisdom.

13. I am patient and kind to myself as I work toward my health goals.

14. I release habits that do not serve my well-being.

15. I am consistent in caring for my body and mind.

16. I feel energized and alive in my daily life.

17. My mental health is just as important as my physical health.

18. I am worthy of feeling balanced and whole.

19. I choose to move my body in ways that feel good to me.

20. I release stress and invite peace into my life.

21. I am grateful for my body and all that it allows me to do.

22. I treat my body with love, care, and compassion.

23. I am in tune with what my body needs to thrive.

24. I choose wellness and joy every day.

25. I am kind to myself, even on days when I don't feel my best.

26. I make time for activities that nourish my mind and soul.

27. I create healthy habits that support my long-term well-being.

28. I trust my ability to make choices that improve my health.

29. My body is strong, resilient, and full of life.

30. I let go of guilt and make self-care a priority.

31. I deserve to feel calm, centered, and at peace.

32. I breathe deeply and allow relaxation to fill my body.

33. My health is a reflection of the love I give to myself.

34. I am grateful for the strength and vitality of my body.

35. I choose to focus on what my body can do, not what it cannot.

36. I am proud of the small steps I take toward better health.

37. My self-care is an investment in my happiness.

38. I create routines that nurture my body and mind.

39. I am worthy of a life filled with energy and vitality.

40. I release negative thoughts about my body and replace them with love.

41. I celebrate the unique beauty of my body.

42. I listen to my body and honor its signals.

43. I trust my body to guide me toward wellness.

44. I am deserving of care, rest, and recovery.

45. I embrace movement as a way to celebrate my body.

46. I make time for stillness and reflection each day.

47. I prioritize my mental health and seek balance in all areas of life.

48. My body thrives when I treat it with love and respect.

49. I choose to let go of habits that do not serve me.

50. I surround myself with people who encourage and support my well-being.

51. I am grateful for every breath and heartbeat.

52. I allow myself to enjoy the process of becoming healthier.

53. I am confident in my ability to create a healthy lifestyle.

54. I forgive myself for any past neglect of my health.

55. I choose progress over perfection in my wellness journey.

56. I treat my body as a sacred and cherished vessel.

57. I am grateful for the energy that flows through me.

58. I release stress and invite calm into my day.

59. I am committed to caring for my mind, body, and spirit.

60. My health is a priority, and I protect it fiercely.

61. I am patient and gentle with myself as I grow.

62. I find joy in nourishing my body with healthy foods.

63. I celebrate the strength and resilience of my body.

64. I am grateful for the healing power of rest.

65. I allow myself to take breaks when needed without guilt.

66. I am mindful of the choices I make for my health.

67. I let go of self-criticism and embrace self-compassion.

68. I am proud of the way I care for myself every day.

69. I choose to prioritize activities that bring me joy and relaxation.

70. My well-being is an important part of my happiness.

71. I am strong enough to make the changes I need for better health.

72. I am grateful for the opportunity to grow healthier each day.

73. I honor my need for balance and take steps to maintain it.

74. I am worthy of feeling vibrant, energized, and alive.

75. I trust the journey of my wellness, even when it feels slow.

76. I am committed to treating my body with love and care.

77. I find peace in taking care of myself.

78. I celebrate the progress I've made in my health journey.

79. I make decisions that align with my long-term wellness goals.

80. I deserve to feel happy, healthy, and whole.

81. I am grateful for the ability to move, breathe, and live fully.

82. I trust my body's ability to heal and recover.

83. I release the need to rush my wellness journey.

84. I find joy in creating healthy routines for myself.

85. I am deserving of the time and energy I dedicate to my well-being.

86. I celebrate the small victories in my health journey.

87. I let go of stress and embrace peace in my mind and body.

88. I am proud of the way I care for my health and happiness.

89. I allow myself to rest without guilt or shame.

90. I choose to focus on what makes me feel healthy and strong.

91. I am capable of creating a life of balance and wellness.

92. I am kind to myself and my body every day.

93. I trust that my body is working for my highest good.

94. I am grateful for the strength and energy I feel today.

95. I celebrate the steps I take to improve my well-being.

96. I am confident in my ability to achieve my health goals.

97. I release any negative thoughts about my wellness journey.

98. I am proud of the effort I put into caring for myself.

99. I choose to nourish my body with love and intention.

100. My health is a reflection of the love I give myself.

101. I create space in my life for peace and stillness.

102. I am worthy of a life filled with vitality and balance.

103. I find joy in taking care of my body and mind.

104. I am grateful for the progress I've made in my wellness journey.

105. I let go of stress and embrace calmness and relaxation.

106. I am confident in my ability to maintain a healthy lifestyle.

107. I honor my body's needs with care and attention.

108. I trust myself to make the best choices for my well-being.

109. I am grateful for the strength and energy I have today.

110. I celebrate every step I take toward better health.

111. I choose to focus on what makes me feel whole and well.

112. I trust the process of creating a balanced and healthy life.

113. I allow myself to rest and recharge without guilt.

114. I am proud of the way I care for my health and wellness.

115. My health is a priority, and I honor it every day.

116. I am committed to loving and nurturing my body.

117. I trust my body's natural ability to heal and thrive.

118. I find peace and joy in taking care of myself.

119. I am grateful for the opportunity to improve my well-being.

120. I honor my need for balance and make choices that reflect it.

121. I am deserving of the love and care I give myself.

122. I am proud of the healthy habits I am building.

123. I trust myself to make the right choices for my health.

124. I celebrate my unique journey toward wellness.

125. I find joy in the process of becoming healthier.

126. I am strong, capable, and committed to my health.

127. I release guilt and embrace self-care as essential.

128. I am worthy of a life filled with energy and vitality.

129. I trust the small steps I take to create a healthier life.

130. I celebrate my progress and look forward to what's next.

131. I make time for rest and rejuvenation in my life.

132. I am grateful for the balance and peace in my life.

133. I honor my body by making choices that support my wellness.

134. I trust the process of healing and growing healthier.

135. I am proud of the way I prioritize my health and happiness.

136. I release stress and allow peace to flow through me.

137. I choose to nourish my body with love and care.

138. I am confident in my ability to create a life of wellness.

139. I celebrate the strength and resilience of my mind and body.

140. I trust that my journey toward health is unfolding perfectly.

141. I am grateful for the opportunity to improve my health.

142. I honor my need for balance and make it a priority.

143. I am proud of the healthy habits I practice every day.

144. I release guilt and allow myself to rest and recharge.

145. I trust myself to make choices that align with my wellness goals.

146. I celebrate my unique journey toward a healthier life.

147. I am committed to loving and nurturing myself fully.

148. I am strong, resilient, and dedicated to my well-being.

149. I release any doubts about my ability to achieve my health goals.

150. I am proud of the effort I put into becoming the healthiest version of myself.

Reflection Prompt:

Which affirmation spoke directly to your current wellness journey? Write it down and use it as a guide throughout your day, reflecting on how it motivates you to take small, meaningful actions toward your health goals.

Health and wellness are lifelong journeys, and every step you take matters. Let these affirmations remind you of your strength, resilience, and the importance of prioritizing your well-being. Let's continue building on this foundation of self-care and balance. Onward to the next chapter!

CHAPTER 7:
AFFIRMATIONS FOR OVERCOMING CHALLENGES AND BUILDING RESILIENCE

"Failure is a great teacher and, if you are open to it, every mistake has a lesson to offer."
—Ruby Dee

Life has a way of testing our limits, pushing us into uncomfortable spaces, and throwing challenges our way when we least expect them. But with every challenge comes an opportunity to grow stronger, to learn, and to discover just how resilient we truly are.

Ruby Dee's words remind us that while failure is a part of life, it's the act of trying—of rising after each fall and learning from it—that defines resilience. This chapter is here to inspire you to persevere, no matter what obstacles stand in your way. These affirmations are a reminder that challenges are not roadblocks; they are stepping stones to becoming the best version of yourself.

Let these affirmations be your foundation when life feels overwhelming. Speak them into existence, and let them guide you toward strength, courage, and an unwavering belief in your ability to rise.

150 Affirmations for Overcoming Challenges and Building Resilience

1. I am stronger than any challenge I face.

2. I rise above difficulties with grace and determination.

3. I am resilient and capable of overcoming anything.

4. I see challenges as opportunities for growth and learning.

5. I trust my ability to navigate life's obstacles.

6. I release fear and embrace courage in difficult times.

7. I am proud of how far I have come, no matter the setbacks.

8. I have the strength to persevere and thrive.

9. I am resourceful and find solutions to every problem.

10. I face challenges head-on with confidence and determination.

11. I let go of self-doubt and trust in my abilities.

12. I am adaptable and open to new ways of overcoming challenges.

13. Every challenge I face builds my resilience and strength.

14. I have the power to turn setbacks into comebacks.

15. I am not defined by my failures but by how I rise after them.

16. I am patient with myself as I work through life's challenges.

17. I trust that every obstacle is teaching me something valuable.

18. I am courageous, even in the face of uncertainty.

19. I embrace the lessons that come from difficult situations.

20. I am stronger than I was yesterday.

21. I release the need to control everything and trust the process.

22. I am proud of the effort I put into overcoming obstacles.

23. I choose to focus on solutions rather than problems.

24. I am capable of achieving great things, no matter the challenges.

25. I trust my inner strength to guide me through tough times.

26. I am resilient, and I bounce back stronger after every setback.

27. I am open to growth, even when it feels uncomfortable.

28. I have the courage to try again after I stumble.

29. I trust that I am exactly where I need to be, even in hard times.

30. I release fear and welcome strength into my heart.

31. I am proud of my ability to face challenges with courage.

32. I am capable of finding peace, even in chaos.

33. I am stronger than the fears that try to hold me back.

34. I trust that the difficulties I face are shaping me for the better.

35. I am brave enough to step outside my comfort zone.

36. I am resilient, resourceful, and determined.

37. I release doubt and trust in my ability to succeed.

38. I find strength in knowing I have overcome challenges before.

39. I am grateful for the lessons that come from life's obstacles.

40. I approach challenges with curiosity and determination.

41. I am proud of my ability to persevere through tough times.

42. I let go of fear and replace it with faith in myself.

43. I am confident in my ability to rise above any challenge.

44. I trust that every setback is setting me up for a comeback.

45. I am capable of turning struggles into strengths.

46. I choose to see difficulties as opportunities for growth.

47. I am fearless in the pursuit of my goals, no matter the obstacles.

48. I embrace change and trust in my ability to adapt.

49. I am resilient and find solutions to every challenge I face.

50. I trust that life's challenges are shaping me into a stronger person.

51. I am grateful for the strength I gain through adversity.

52. I choose to focus on the lessons, not the difficulties.

53. I release the fear of failure and embrace the courage to try.

54. I am capable of finding light in even the darkest moments.

55. I am patient with myself as I navigate life's challenges.

56. I trust my ability to overcome anything that comes my way.

57. I release self-doubt and replace it with self-belief.

58. I am proud of the way I handle life's challenges.

59. I choose to focus on progress, not perfection.

60. I am resilient and grow stronger with each challenge I face.

61. I trust that I have the tools to overcome any obstacle.

62. I let go of fear and embrace confidence in tough situations.

63. I am stronger than I realize and braver than I know.

64. I face challenges with an open heart and mind.

65. I trust that everything I need is already within me.

66. I am capable of creating solutions in even the hardest times.

67. I am proud of my ability to keep going, no matter what.

68. I choose to rise above challenges with strength and grace.

69. I trust that I am exactly where I need to be to grow.

70. I let go of worry and replace it with trust in myself.

71. I am proud of the resilience I show in difficult times.

72. I embrace every challenge as an opportunity to learn.

73. I trust my ability to handle anything life throws my way.

74. I am strong enough to face my fears and overcome them.

75. I am resilient and capable of achieving my goals.

76. I release negativity and focus on the positive in every situation.

77. I am grateful for the opportunity to grow through adversity.

78. I choose to see every challenge as a stepping stone to success.

79. I am capable of finding strength in even the hardest moments.

80. I trust that I am being prepared for something greater.

81. I am confident in my ability to adapt to change.

82. I am proud of the effort I put into overcoming challenges.

83. I am open to learning from every obstacle I face.

84. I am strong, resilient, and determined to succeed.

85. I trust my ability to rise above any hardship.

86. I let go of fear and replace it with unwavering courage.

87. I am grateful for the strength I gain from overcoming difficulties.

88. I choose to focus on the progress I make each day.

89. I am proud of the resilience I build through challenges.

90. I embrace change as a necessary part of growth.

91. I trust my instincts to guide me through tough times.

92. I am capable of turning setbacks into opportunities for growth.

93. I choose to rise above adversity with grace and strength.

94. I am confident in my ability to face any challenge head-on.

95. I trust that every challenge is teaching me something valuable.

96. I am proud of the strength I show in overcoming obstacles.

97. I am resilient and capable of achieving great things.

98. I release fear and embrace courage in every situation.

99. I am grateful for the lessons that come from difficult times.

100. I choose to see every difficulty as a chance to grow.

101. I am confident in my ability to overcome any challenge.

102. I trust that every setback is an opportunity for a comeback.

103. I am resilient, resourceful, and determined to succeed.

104. I let go of worry and trust the process of growth.

105. I am strong enough to face any fear and conquer it.

106. I am proud of my ability to rise above difficulties.

107. I trust that every challenge is shaping me for the better.

108. I embrace resilience as a part of who I am.

109. I choose to focus on solutions, not problems.

110. I am fearless in the face of uncertainty.

111. I trust my strength to guide me through life's challenges.

112. I am grateful for the resilience I gain through adversity.

113. I release fear and replace it with confidence.

114. I am proud of the way I handle life's difficulties.

115. I am capable of finding light in even the darkest moments.

116. I trust that every obstacle is helping me grow.

117. I am confident in my ability to persevere through tough times.

118. I am proud of the progress I make every day.

119. I embrace challenges as opportunities to grow stronger.

120. I trust that I have everything I need to overcome adversity.

121. I release self-doubt and replace it with self-belief.

122. I am grateful for the lessons I learn through challenges.

123. I choose to rise above every obstacle with strength.

124. I trust that I am capable of overcoming anything.

125. I am resilient and find solutions to every problem.

126. I am confident in my ability to navigate life's challenges.

127. I am proud of my courage to face life's obstacles.

128. I trust that my strength will carry me through any hardship.

129. I release negativity and embrace positivity in tough times.

130. I am grateful for the strength I gain through adversity.

131. I choose to see challenges as opportunities for success.

132. I trust that I am being prepared for something greater.

133. I am resilient and capable of achieving my dreams.

134. I am confident in my ability to overcome any hardship.

135. I am proud of my ability to face challenges with courage.

136. I trust that I am growing stronger with every obstacle I overcome.

137. I release fear and replace it with unwavering faith in myself.

138. I am grateful for the lessons I learn through life's challenges.

139. I am proud of the resilience I show in tough times.

140. I choose to focus on growth, not setbacks.

141. I trust my instincts to guide me through adversity.

142. I am capable of turning difficulties into opportunities for growth.

143. I embrace every challenge as a chance to learn.

144. I am resilient and determined to achieve my goals.

145. I am confident in my ability to rise above every difficulty.

146. I trust that every obstacle is helping me become stronger.

147. I am proud of the progress I make in overcoming challenges.

148. I release fear and embrace confidence in tough situations.

149. I am resilient, resourceful, and capable of great things.

150. I am grateful for the opportunity to grow through adversity.

REFLECTION PROMPT:

What challenge are you currently facing? Choose one affirmation that speaks directly to your situation and repeat it daily. Let it remind you of your strength and resilience as you navigate this moment.

Resilience isn't about never falling; it's about always rising. Let these affirmations serve as a steady foundation as you face life's challenges with courage and determination. Together, let's move forward to the next chapter.

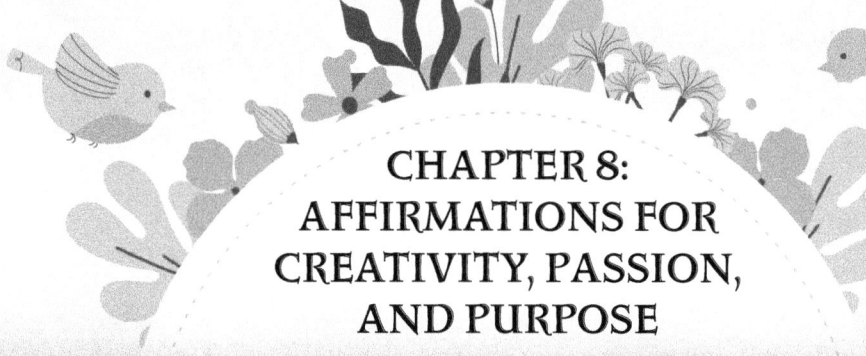

CHAPTER 8:
AFFIRMATIONS FOR CREATIVITY, PASSION, AND PURPOSE

"You can't use up creativity. The more you use, the more you have."
—Maya Angelou

Creativity is a force that lives within all of us. It's not limited to artists, writers, or musicians—it's in how we solve problems, envision new possibilities, and express who we are. When creativity is aligned with passion and purpose, it becomes one of the most powerful tools for living a fulfilling life.

Maya Angelou's words remind us that creativity is infinite—it grows as we nurture and use it. Whether you're pursuing a personal passion, building a career, or simply exploring new ways to bring joy into your life, these affirmations are designed to unlock your creative potential and align you with your purpose.

This chapter invites you to embrace your unique gifts, trust your instincts, and step boldly into a life fueled by creativity, passion, and meaning.

150 Affirmations for Creativity, Passion, and Purpose

1. I am a creative being with endless ideas and inspiration.

2. I trust my unique talents and use them with confidence.

3. My creativity flows effortlessly and abundantly.

4. I am passionate about the work I do and the life I create.

5. I am aligned with my purpose and follow it with joy.

6. I honor my passions and make time to nurture them.

7. I allow my creativity to guide me to new opportunities.

8. I am proud of the originality I bring to everything I do.

9. I trust that my purpose is unfolding exactly as it should.

10. My creative ideas are valuable and worth pursuing.

11. I am fearless in expressing my creativity.

12. I trust my instincts to guide me toward meaningful work.

13. My passion fuels my determination and drive.

14. I am open to exploring new ideas and perspectives.

15. My creativity knows no limits or boundaries.

16. I am confident in my ability to create something meaningful.

17. I allow myself the freedom to dream big and take risks.

18. I embrace my creative potential with excitement and gratitude.

19. I am inspired by the world around me and within me.

20. I trust that my passions will lead me to success.

21. My purpose is unique, and I honor it fully.

22. I am a source of inspiration to others through my creativity.

23. I find joy in expressing myself authentically.

24. I am open to new opportunities that align with my passions.

25. I trust the process of creating, even when it feels uncertain.

26. I am capable of turning my dreams into reality.

27. I embrace the challenges that come with pursuing my purpose.

28. I am grateful for the creative energy that flows through me.

29. I trust that my creativity will lead me to incredible possibilities.

30. I am passionate about the life I am building for myself.

31. My purpose lights the way toward fulfillment and happiness.

32. I am not afraid to explore new ways of expressing myself.

33. I am committed to using my creativity to make a difference.

34. My unique perspective is a gift to the world.

35. I am proud of the originality I bring to every project.

36. I allow myself to explore my passions without fear or doubt.

37. I trust that my purpose is always evolving in beautiful ways.

38. I am bold in pursuing what sets my soul on fire.

39. My creativity brings me joy, freedom, and peace.

40. I am grateful for the opportunities to express my passions.

41. I embrace the journey of discovering and living my purpose.

42. I allow my creativity to flow without judgment or fear.

43. I trust that my ideas are valuable and worth sharing.

44. I am passionate about the process of creating and growing.

45. I trust my instincts to guide me toward meaningful work.

46. My purpose brings clarity and direction to my life.

47. I am open to inspiration from unexpected places.

48. I am proud of the creative solutions I bring to challenges.

49. I allow my creativity to grow and evolve naturally.

50. I am passionate about exploring new possibilities.

51. I trust that my talents are leading me to a fulfilling life.

52. My creativity is a source of joy and empowerment.

53. I embrace my unique gifts and share them freely.

54. I am not afraid to take bold steps toward my dreams.

55. I am confident in my ability to create something extraordinary.

56. My passion inspires me to keep moving forward.

57. I allow my creativity to flow without hesitation or fear.

58. I trust that my purpose is aligned with my deepest desires.

59. I am grateful for the clarity and passion I feel about my work.

60. I honor my creative process, even when it feels messy.

61. I am open to experimenting and trying new things.

62. I trust my ability to bring my ideas to life.

63. My creativity is a reflection of my inner beauty and strength.

64. I am passionate about making a positive impact through my work.

65. My purpose is my compass, guiding me toward fulfillment.

66. I am proud of the risks I take in the name of my dreams.

67. I allow my passions to fuel my persistence and courage.

68. I trust that my unique talents will create opportunities for me.

69. My creativity grows stronger with every new idea I explore.

70. I am passionate about living a life of purpose and meaning.

71. I honor my creative instincts and trust where they lead me.

72. I am proud of the originality I bring to everything I create.

73. I allow myself to embrace the joy of creating.

74. I trust that my passions will guide me toward success.

75. I am committed to pursuing my purpose, no matter what.

76. My creativity is a source of healing and empowerment.

77. I am open to exploring new paths that align with my purpose.

78. I trust that my ideas are valuable and worth pursuing.

79. I am proud of the passion I bring to every aspect of my life.

80. I allow my creativity to flow without limitations.

81. I trust that my purpose is always evolving in beautiful ways.

82. I embrace the unknown as part of the creative process.

83. I am confident in my ability to bring my ideas to life.

84. My passion is my guide, leading me to new opportunities.

85. I am proud of the courage it takes to follow my dreams.

86. I allow my creativity to shine brightly in everything I do.

87. I trust that my purpose is guiding me toward fulfillment.

88. I am passionate about sharing my gifts with the world.

89. I honor the creative process and trust its timing.

90. My creativity is limitless, and I embrace its power.

91. I am committed to living a life that aligns with my purpose.

92. I trust my instincts to guide me toward meaningful work.

93. I am proud of the unique perspective I bring to the world.

94. I allow my creativity to flourish without fear of failure.

95. I trust that my passion will lead me to extraordinary experiences.

96. My purpose gives me clarity and direction in life.

97. I am grateful for the creative energy that flows through me.

98. I embrace the freedom and joy of expressing myself.

99. I am confident in my ability to make my dreams a reality.

100. My creativity is a reflection of my authentic self.

101. I trust that my talents are guiding me toward a fulfilling life.

102. I am proud of the originality I bring to every project.

103. I allow my passions to inspire and motivate me daily.

104. I trust my purpose to guide me toward true fulfillment.

105. I embrace the challenges that come with pursuing my dreams.

106. I am confident in my ability to create something meaningful.

107. My creativity inspires me to keep growing and evolving.

108. I am passionate about the process of creating and discovering.

109. I honor my purpose by taking bold steps forward.

110. My creativity is infinite, and I embrace its abundance.

111. I trust that my ideas will lead me to incredible opportunities.

112. I am proud of the courage it takes to follow my passion.

113. I allow my creativity to guide me toward new adventures.

114. My passion fuels my determination to succeed.

115. I trust that my purpose will always lead me toward joy.

116. I am grateful for the clarity and passion I feel about my work.

117. I honor the unique path my creativity takes me on.

118. My creativity is a gift, and I share it freely.

119. I trust my instincts to guide me toward meaningful work.

120. I am passionate about making a difference through my creativity.

121. My purpose brings clarity and fulfillment to my life.

122. I am proud of the risks I take in pursuit of my dreams.

123. I allow my creativity to flow without judgment.

124. I trust my talents to create a life of joy and purpose.

125. I am confident in my ability to bring my ideas to fruition.

126. My creativity grows stronger with every challenge I face.

127. I am passionate about living a life filled with purpose.

128. I honor my passions and trust where they lead me.

129. I am proud of the originality I bring to every aspect of my life.

130. I allow my creativity to flow naturally and effortlessly.

131. I trust that my purpose will always guide me toward fulfillment.

132. My passion inspires me to take bold steps forward.

133. I embrace the journey of pursuing my dreams with excitement.

134. I am grateful for the creative energy that flows through me daily.

135. My creativity brings me joy and fulfillment in everything I do.

136. I trust my instincts to guide me toward meaningful opportunities.

137. I am passionate about sharing my talents with the world.

138. My purpose brings clarity and direction to my life.

139. I am proud of the creativity I bring to every challenge.

140. I allow my passions to guide me toward a life of meaning.

141. My creativity inspires me to dream bigger and aim higher.

142. I trust that my purpose is always unfolding beautifully.

143. I am confident in my ability to create something extraordinary.

144. My passion fuels my courage to take risks and grow.

145. I honor my creative process and trust its flow.

146. My creativity is infinite, and I embrace its abundance.

147. I trust that my talents are leading me to success and joy.

148. I am proud of the originality I bring to every project I pursue.

149. I allow my creativity to flourish in every area of my life.

150. My purpose is clear, and I follow it with passion and determination.

REFLECTION PROMPT:

What area of your life would benefit most from a spark of creativity or a deeper connection to purpose? Choose an affirmation that speaks to this need and use it as your guide today.

Creativity, passion, and purpose are intertwined—they fuel one another and create a life that feels vibrant and meaningful. Let these affirmations remind you of your unique gifts and inspire you to live boldly and authentically. Let's move forward to the next chapter.

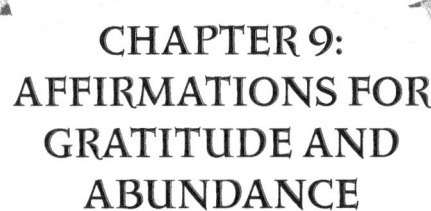

CHAPTER 9:
AFFIRMATIONS FOR GRATITUDE AND ABUNDANCE

"Thank you expresses extreme gratitude, humility, understanding."
—Alice Walker

Gratitude is a transformative practice. It shifts your perspective from what's missing in your life to the abundance that already surrounds you. When you live with gratitude, you attract even more reasons to be thankful. It opens the door for abundance—not just financial, but also in love, joy, opportunities, and peace.

This chapter is an invitation to embrace the power of gratitude. These affirmations are here to help you cultivate a heart full of thankfulness, no matter the season of life you're in. By focusing on the abundance that's already present, you'll begin to see even more of it unfolding in your life.

150 Affirmations for Gratitude and Abundance

1. I am deeply grateful for the life I have.

2. I see abundance in every area of my life.

3. I am thankful for the simple joys that fill my day.

4. I wake up each morning with a heart full of gratitude.

5. I choose to focus on the good that surrounds me.

6. I am grateful for the lessons that life has taught me.

7. I attract abundance by appreciating what I already have.

8. My heart is open to receiving all of life's blessings.

9. I am thankful for the love and support in my life.

10. Gratitude is my default state of mind.

11. I appreciate the beauty of the world around me.

12. I am grateful for every opportunity to grow and learn.

13. I welcome abundance into my life with open arms.

14. I am thankful for the people who bring joy to my life.

15. I celebrate the abundance that flows freely to me.

16. I am grateful for the challenges that have made me stronger.

17. My heart is filled with gratitude for today's blessings.

18. I am thankful for the breath that fills my lungs.

19. I see the beauty in every moment and give thanks.

20. I attract abundance by radiating gratitude and joy.

21. I am grateful for the opportunities that come my way.

22. My gratitude multiplies the blessings in my life.

23. I choose to see challenges as opportunities for growth.

24. I am thankful for the abundance of love in my life.

25. I appreciate the small things that make life beautiful.

26. My life is overflowing with reasons to be thankful.

27. I am grateful for the support of my friends and family.

28. I embrace gratitude as a daily practice.

29. I am thankful for the wisdom I gain through experience.

30. My gratitude attracts even more abundance into my life.

31. I am grateful for the gift of being alive.

32. I see abundance everywhere I look.

33. I am thankful for the kindness of others.

34. I appreciate the lessons I've learned from difficult times.

35. My heart is full of gratitude for the good in my life.

36. I am thankful for the opportunities to create my dreams.

37. I embrace every moment with a thankful heart.

38. I appreciate the abundance of nature that surrounds me.

39. I am grateful for the ability to create positive change.

40. I am thankful for the love I receive and the love I give.

41. My life is rich with blessings, and I acknowledge them daily.

42. I am grateful for the opportunities to make a difference.

43. I am thankful for the abundance that flows effortlessly to me.

44. I celebrate the progress I have made on my journey.

45. I see every day as an opportunity to practice gratitude.

46. I appreciate the abundance of possibilities in my life.

47. I am grateful for the relationships that bring joy and growth.

48. I am thankful for the comfort and safety of my home.

49. I choose to focus on what I have, not what I lack.

50. I embrace gratitude as a tool for attracting abundance.

51. I am thankful for the experiences that have shaped me.

52. My gratitude grows with every breath I take.

53. I am grateful for the endless opportunities to love and be loved.

54. I celebrate the abundance of blessings in my life.

55. I am thankful for my health and well-being.

56. I appreciate the abundance of resources available to me.

57. My heart is filled with gratitude for life's simple pleasures.

58. I am thankful for the kindness I see in the world.

59. I attract abundance by living with a grateful heart.

60. I am grateful for the abundance of time to enjoy life's moments.

61. I appreciate the unique blessings each day brings.

62. My life is enriched by my gratitude.

63. I am thankful for the beauty of each sunrise and sunset.

64. I am grateful for the love that surrounds me.

65. I choose to see every challenge as an opportunity to grow.

66. I am thankful for the strength I have to overcome obstacles.

67. I appreciate the abundance of joy in my life.

68. My gratitude is a magnet for positive experiences.

69. I am grateful for the freedom to create my future.

70. I celebrate the abundance of opportunities before me.

71. I am thankful for the people who inspire and uplift me.

72. I am grateful for the abundance of laughter in my life.

73. My heart is full of gratitude for the lessons I've learned.

74. I choose to see the abundance in every situation.

75. I am thankful for the beauty of the present moment.

76. I appreciate the abundance of choices available to me.

77. My gratitude fuels my happiness and peace.

78. I am grateful for the courage to pursue my dreams.

79. I celebrate the abundance of love in my relationships.

80. I am thankful for the opportunities to grow and evolve.

81. I see the abundance of good in the world around me.

82. My heart is filled with gratitude for my journey.

83. I am grateful for the abundance of possibilities in my life.

84. I appreciate the people who bring joy and support to my life.

85. I am thankful for the opportunities to express my creativity.

86. My gratitude creates a ripple effect of positivity.

87. I embrace every moment with a thankful heart.

88. I am grateful for the abundance of happiness in my life.

89. My heart overflows with gratitude for today's blessings.

90. I am thankful for the freedom to live authentically.

91. I appreciate the abundance of inspiration in my life.

92. My gratitude attracts even more reasons to be thankful.

93. I am grateful for the progress I've made toward my goals.

94. I celebrate the abundance of peace in my heart.

95. I am thankful for the opportunities to share my gifts.

96. I am grateful for the abundance of knowledge I've gained.

97. My gratitude opens the door to unlimited possibilities.

98. I am thankful for the love and connection in my life.

99. I embrace gratitude as a way of life.

100. My heart is full of gratitude for the journey I'm on.

101. I see abundance in every area of my life.

102. I am thankful for the support and encouragement I receive.

103. My gratitude creates space for even greater blessings.

104. I appreciate the abundance of beauty in the world.

105. I am grateful for the lessons that help me grow.

106. My heart is filled with gratitude for life's endless possibilities.

107. I am thankful for the strength and resilience I possess.

108. I celebrate the abundance of laughter and joy in my days.

109. I am grateful for the clarity and peace I feel.

110. My gratitude amplifies the abundance in my life.

111. I am thankful for the chance to make a positive impact.

112. I appreciate the abundance of energy and motivation I feel.

113. My heart is full of gratitude for the life I'm building.

114. I celebrate the abundance of opportunities to learn and grow.

115. I am thankful for the love and kindness I receive each day.

116. I embrace the abundance of possibilities in my future.

117. My gratitude makes every moment richer and more meaningful.

118. I am thankful for the abundance of joy in the little things.

119. I celebrate the progress I've made toward my dreams.

120. I am grateful for the abundance of support in my life.

121. My heart is full of gratitude for the beauty of today.

122. I am thankful for the opportunities to create a fulfilling life.

123. I appreciate the abundance of strength and courage within me.

124. My gratitude fills my life with happiness and peace.

125. I celebrate the abundance of blessings I've been given.

126. I am grateful for the opportunity to start fresh each day.

127. My heart overflows with gratitude for the people I love.

128. I am thankful for the abundance of hope in my life.

129. I appreciate the beauty and abundance of nature.

130. My gratitude creates more space for love and joy.

131. I am grateful for the abundance of inspiration that surrounds me.

132. I celebrate the abundance of creativity in my work.

133. I am thankful for the opportunity to make a difference.

134. My gratitude strengthens my relationships with others.

135. I appreciate the abundance of peace in my heart.

136. I am grateful for the abundance of wisdom I've gained.

137. My heart is full of gratitude for the journey I'm on.

138. I celebrate the abundance of kindness in the world.

139. I am thankful for the chance to live fully and authentically.

140. My gratitude enriches every aspect of my life.

141. I embrace the abundance of opportunities before me.

142. I am grateful for the love and connection I experience daily.

143. I appreciate the abundance of growth and learning in my life.

144. My heart is full of gratitude for the progress I've made.

145. I celebrate the abundance of love I feel in my relationships.

146. I am thankful for the strength to overcome challenges.

147. I appreciate the abundance of joy in the present moment.

148. My gratitude fuels my happiness and optimism.

149. I am grateful for the opportunities to live my best life.

150. My heart is overflowing with gratitude for the abundance around me.

REFLECTION PROMPT:

What is one thing you're deeply grateful for today? Write it down and reflect on how it brings abundance into your life. Let that gratitude fuel you throughout the day.

Living with gratitude transforms your perspective and opens the door to endless abundance. These affirmations are here to remind you of the blessings you already have and to welcome even more into your life. Let's continue to the next chapter.

CHAPTER 10:
AFFIRMATIONS FOR
CONFIDENCE AND
SELF-EMPOWERMENT

"The most common way people give up their power is by thinking they don't have any."
—Alice Walker

Confidence and self-empowerment are at the heart of personal growth. They allow you to take ownership of your life, make decisions with clarity, and show up fully and unapologetically. Often, we unknowingly give away our power by doubting ourselves or allowing fear to dictate our actions. Alice Walker's words remind us that true power begins with acknowledging that it's already within us.

This chapter is designed to help you tap into your confidence, reclaim your personal power, and walk boldly in your truth. These affirmations will remind you of your strength, your worth, and your ability to create the life you envision. Speak them with intention and let them inspire you to step into your power unapologetically.

150 Affirmations for Confidence and Self-Empowerment

1. I am confident in who I am and what I bring to the world.

2. I trust my intuition to guide me toward what is best for me.

3. I am fearless in expressing my thoughts and opinions.

4. My confidence grows stronger with every decision I make.

5. I am proud of the person I am becoming.

6. I walk through life with purpose and clarity.

7. I am in control of my thoughts, emotions, and actions.

8. I embrace my uniqueness and celebrate my individuality.

9. I am worthy of success, love, and happiness.

10. My voice matters, and I use it with courage and conviction.

11. I trust myself to handle whatever comes my way.

12. I am capable of achieving anything I set my mind to.

13. I let go of self-doubt and fully embrace my power.

14. I am proud of my resilience and inner strength.

15. I show up confidently in every area of my life.

16. I release the need for validation from others and trust myself.

17. I am strong, capable, and unstoppable.

18. My confidence inspires those around me.

19. I am bold and courageous in the pursuit of my dreams.

20. I honor my boundaries as an act of self-respect.

21. I am deserving of all the success and joy I envision for myself.

22. I trust my ability to create the life I desire.

23. I am proud of how far I've come and excited for what's ahead.

24. I let go of fear and step boldly into new opportunities.

25. I am a powerful force for good in my own life.

26. I embrace challenges as opportunities to grow and learn.

27. I am confident in my ability to navigate any situation.

28. My confidence radiates from within and uplifts me.

29. I am in charge of my happiness and fulfillment.

30. I am not afraid to take up space and be heard.

31. I am proud of the unique talents and gifts I bring to the world.

32. I am strong enough to overcome any obstacle.

33. I trust my instincts and honor my inner wisdom.

34. I am confident in my ability to make decisions that serve me.

35. I choose to see myself as powerful, capable, and worthy.

36. My confidence grows with every step I take toward my goals.

37. I release the fear of failure and embrace the courage to try.

38. I am proud of the progress I make every day.

39. I trust that I am exactly where I need to be in my journey.

40. I am fearless in pursuing what sets my soul on fire.

41. My confidence opens doors to new opportunities and experiences.

42. I am proud of my ability to stand up for myself and my beliefs.

43. I trust myself to overcome any challenge that comes my way.

44. I release self-doubt and replace it with unwavering self-belief.

45. I am confident in my ability to inspire and uplift others.

46. I am worthy of the dreams I envision for myself.

47. I embrace my power and use it to create a meaningful life.

48. I am proud of the courage it takes to step out of my comfort zone.

49. I trust my ability to turn obstacles into opportunities.

50. I choose confidence over fear and self-doubt.

51. I am deserving of respect and appreciation in every aspect of my life.

52. I am strong enough to set and maintain healthy boundaries.

53. My confidence inspires me to take bold and meaningful action.

54. I trust my journey and the lessons it brings.

55. I am capable of achieving greatness in my own unique way.

56. I embrace the power of my voice and speak my truth confidently.

57. I am proud of the person I see when I look in the mirror.

58. I let go of limiting beliefs and embrace my potential.

59. My confidence grows stronger with every choice I make.

60. I am fearless in facing the unknown and embracing new beginnings.

61. I trust that I am capable of handling whatever life brings my way.

62. I am deserving of the success I work hard to achieve.

63. I am confident in my ability to learn, grow, and adapt.

64. I release comparison and embrace my unique journey.

65. I am proud of the strength and resilience I carry within me.

66. I am bold enough to pursue my passions without hesitation.

67. I trust my ability to make the best choices for my life.

68. My confidence empowers me to create the future I desire.

69. I am strong, capable, and deserving of every good thing.

70. I let go of fear and embrace the courage to stand tall.

71. I am proud of the way I show up for myself every day.

72. I trust that my path is leading me toward fulfillment and joy.

73. I am confident in my ability to face and conquer challenges.

74. My self-worth is not determined by the opinions of others.

75. I am proud of my ability to grow and evolve through life's experiences.

76. I embrace my power and use it to create a positive impact.

77. I trust myself to make decisions that align with my values.

78. I am confident in my ability to achieve my goals and dreams.

79. I let go of fear and step boldly into new opportunities.

80. I am strong enough to navigate any storm with grace.

81. My confidence radiates positivity and strength.

82. I am proud of my ability to persevere through challenges.

83. I trust my intuition to guide me toward the best outcomes.

84. I am fearless in pursuing my passions and dreams.

85. My self-confidence grows stronger with each passing day.

86. I am deserving of love, success, and happiness in every area of my life.

87. I embrace the power of my choices and their impact on my future.

88. I am proud of the courage it takes to be my authentic self.

89. I trust myself to rise above any challenge or obstacle.

90. My confidence is a reflection of my inner strength and resilience.

91. I am bold enough to live life on my own terms.

92. I am proud of the decisions I make to protect my peace.

93. I trust that I have everything I need to succeed within me.

94. I am confident in my ability to create the life I envision.

95. I let go of fear and step into my power unapologetically.

96. I am strong, resilient, and capable of achieving greatness.

97. My confidence inspires me to take meaningful action every day.

98. I trust that my journey is leading me toward fulfillment and joy.

99. I am fearless in showing up as my authentic self.

100. I am proud of my ability to create a life I love.

101. I am worthy of the love and respect I desire.

102. I trust my ability to learn and grow through every experience.

103. I am confident in my ability to create positive change.

104. I release fear and embrace my natural strengths.

105. I am proud of the courage it takes to pursue my dreams.

106. I trust my instincts to guide me toward the right opportunities.

107. I am deserving of a life filled with confidence and self-belief.

108. I embrace the power within me to achieve my goals.

109. I am fearless in taking bold steps toward my future.

110. My confidence grows stronger with every new challenge I face.

111. I am proud of the resilience I show in difficult moments.

112. I trust that my hard work will lead me to success.

113. I am confident in my ability to overcome any obstacle.

114. My self-worth is a reflection of my inner strength.

115. I am proud of the way I advocate for myself and my needs.

116. I embrace my power and use it to create a meaningful life.

117. I trust my ability to navigate life's ups and downs with grace.

118. My confidence inspires others to believe in themselves.

119. I am deserving of every success I achieve.

120. I am bold enough to stand in my truth and speak my mind.

121. I trust that every step I take brings me closer to my goals.

122. I am confident in my ability to build a life I love.

123. My power lies in my ability to believe in myself fully.

124. I am proud of the strength I show in every situation.

125. I release fear and embrace the confidence within me.

126. I am fearless in taking the next step toward my dreams.

127. I trust that my decisions are leading me toward success.

128. I am proud of the person I am growing into every day.

129. My confidence empowers me to make bold choices.

130. I embrace the challenges that come with stepping into my power.

131. I am fearless in pursuing a life of purpose and passion.

132. I trust my instincts to guide me toward the right path.

133. My self-confidence is unshakable and unwavering.

134. I am proud of the way I show up for myself each day.

135. I release fear and replace it with faith in my abilities.

136. I trust that my strength will carry me through any challenge.

137. I am confident in my ability to create the life I envision.

138. My power lies in my courage to show up authentically.

139. I am proud of the decisions I make to honor myself.

140. I embrace the power of self-belief and determination.

141. I am fearless in creating a life that reflects my values.

142. I trust my intuition to guide me toward what's best for me.

143. My confidence inspires me to take meaningful action.

144. I am bold enough to pursue the life I desire.

145. I am proud of the resilience I show in the face of challenges.

146. I release fear and embrace the confidence to lead my life.

147. I trust my ability to overcome any obstacle with grace.

148. My self-worth is a reflection of my courage and strength.

149. I am proud of the progress I've made in owning my power.

150. I am confident in my ability to create a future filled with joy and success.

REFLECTION PROMPT:

Which affirmation resonates with your current journey toward self-empowerment? Write it down and repeat it to yourself throughout the day. Let it guide your actions and inspire your confidence.

Confidence and self-empowerment come from within. These affirmations are here to help you remember your strength and step boldly into your power. Let's continue to the next chapter, building on this foundation.

CHAPTER 11:
AFFIRMATIONS FOR SPIRITUAL GROWTH AND INNER ALIGNMENT

"When I dare to be powerful, to use my strength in the service of my vision, then it becomes less and less important whether I am afraid."
—Audre Lorde

Spiritual growth is about connecting with your inner self, finding peace within, and aligning your life with your values and purpose. It's not necessarily tied to religion—it's about the deep, personal journey of understanding who you are and how you relate to the world around you. Audre Lorde's words remind us that sometimes we may be afraid of doing things, but we need to step outside of our comfort zone to achieve our visions, aims, and goals.

This chapter is designed to help you nurture your spiritual journey, deepen your self-awareness, and connect with the energy that flows within and around you. These affirmations encourage mindfulness, alignment, and peace as you grow spiritually and embrace the best version of yourself.

150 Affirmations for Spiritual Growth and Inner Alignment

1. I am deeply connected to my inner self and higher purpose.

2. My spiritual growth is a journey I honor and embrace.

3. I trust the wisdom within me to guide my path.

4. I am aligned with the energy of peace and love.

5. I choose to nourish my soul with positivity and purpose.

6. My intuition is a powerful guide, and I trust it fully.

7. I am open to the lessons the universe has for me.

8. I release fear and embrace faith in my journey.

9. My spiritual growth brings me clarity and inner peace.

10. I am grateful for the connection I have with the world around me.

11. I am aligned with the flow of the universe.

12. My soul is calm, and my spirit is at peace.

13. I trust that every step I take is leading me toward alignment.

14. I am open to the beauty of the present moment.

15. My spiritual journey is unique, and I honor its unfolding.

16. I am grounded and centered in my purpose.

17. I trust the process of growth and transformation.

18. I release what no longer serves me and welcome new energy.

19. I am connected to the infinite wisdom of the universe.

20. My spirit is strong, resilient, and unwavering.

21. I embrace the stillness that nurtures my soul.

22. I am at peace with where I am and excited about where I'm going.

23. I trust the divine timing of my life.

24. I am in harmony with my mind, body, and soul.

25. My spiritual practice enriches every aspect of my life.

26. I allow myself to grow through challenges and lessons.

27. I am grateful for the inner strength my spirituality provides.

28. My soul is a source of endless light and love.

29. I release doubt and trust in the unfolding of my journey.

30. I honor the divine energy within me and around me.

31. I am deeply connected to my purpose and calling.

32. My spiritual growth is a reflection of my love for myself.

33. I embrace the journey of self-discovery and growth.

34. I am grateful for the stillness that brings clarity to my soul.

35. I trust the guidance of my inner wisdom.

36. I am open to receiving spiritual guidance and inspiration.

37. My spirit is aligned with the energy of abundance and joy.

38. I release negativity and welcome peace into my heart.

39. I am grounded in the present moment and trust its lessons.

40. I honor my spiritual practice as an act of self-love.

41. My soul is a sanctuary of calm and peace.

42. I am grateful for the spiritual journey that enriches my life.

43. I trust the unfolding of my path, even when it feels uncertain.

44. I release control and allow the universe to guide me.

45. My spiritual growth brings me closer to my true self.

46. I am aligned with the energy of healing and transformation.

47. I embrace the unknown as part of my spiritual journey.

48. My soul is nourished by love, peace, and purpose.

49. I trust that everything I need is already within me.

50. I honor my connection to the divine energy that surrounds me.

51. My spiritual growth is a continuous process of learning and evolving.

52. I release judgment of myself and others, replacing it with compassion.

53. I am open to the wisdom that life's challenges bring.

54. My spirit is at peace, even in the midst of uncertainty.

55. I am grateful for the guidance that flows through my intuition.

56. I trust that my journey is leading me exactly where I need to be.

57. I embrace the balance between my inner and outer worlds.

58. I am aligned with my values, my purpose, and my soul's calling.

59. My spiritual practice is a source of strength and clarity.

60. I release resistance and flow with the energy of the universe.

61. I am grateful for the moments of stillness that nourish my soul.

62. My soul is deeply connected to the rhythm of life.

63. I trust my inner voice to guide me with wisdom and love.

64. I am open to receiving spiritual insight and clarity.

65. My spiritual growth is a reflection of my dedication to self-love.

66. I am in tune with the energy of love, peace, and abundance.

67. I release fear and step into the light of faith and trust.

68. My spirit is resilient, and my heart is open.

69. I am grateful for the journey of growth that enriches my life.

70. I honor the divine within myself and others.

71. My spiritual practice fills me with a sense of purpose and joy.

72. I trust the timing of my spiritual awakening.

73. I am open to the messages the universe sends me.

74. My soul is aligned with the energy of gratitude and love.

75. I release old patterns and embrace new beginnings.

76. My spiritual journey brings me peace, clarity, and joy.

77. I am grounded in the present and trust its purpose.

78. I honor the stillness that allows me to hear my inner voice.

79. My soul is nourished by connection and purpose.

80. I trust the flow of life to guide me toward alignment.

81. I am open to the beauty and mystery of the spiritual journey.

82. I release fear and embrace the power of faith.

83. My spirit is a source of strength, courage, and wisdom.

84. I am grateful for the spiritual energy that flows through me.

85. I honor the journey of self-discovery and growth.

86. My soul is at peace, and my heart is full of love.

87. I trust the divine wisdom that guides my path.

88. I am open to the lessons the universe has for me.

89. My spiritual growth is a source of joy and inspiration.

90. I release doubt and embrace faith in the process.

91. I honor my spiritual journey as a reflection of my inner strength.

92. My spirit is aligned with the energy of healing and love.

93. I trust the stillness to bring clarity and peace to my soul.

94. My soul is deeply connected to the energy of the universe.

95. I embrace the beauty and mystery of spiritual growth.

96. My spiritual journey enriches my life in every way.

97. I release fear and step into the light of love and faith.

98. My heart is open to the peace that spirituality brings.

99. I am grateful for the strength my spiritual practice provides.

100. I honor the journey of growth that brings me closer to my purpose.

101. I trust my inner wisdom to guide me with clarity and love.

102. My soul is nourished by the energy of peace and gratitude.

103. I release negativity and embrace the light of healing.

104. I trust the process of spiritual alignment and growth.

105. My spiritual journey brings me closer to my true self.

106. I honor the lessons that come with life's challenges.

107. My soul is a source of infinite light and love.

108. I am open to the guidance of my intuition and inner voice.

109. My spiritual practice brings me strength, clarity, and peace.

110. I trust the flow of life to guide me toward alignment.

111. My spirit is resilient, and my heart is open to growth.

112. I am grateful for the clarity my spiritual practice provides.

113. I release resistance and trust the unfolding of my path.

114. My soul is deeply connected to the beauty of life.

115. I honor the wisdom that comes from my spiritual journey.

116. I trust my ability to align with my purpose and calling.

117. My spiritual growth is a reflection of my love for myself.

118. I am grounded in the present and open to its lessons.

119. My soul is a sanctuary of calm and peace.

120. I am grateful for the spiritual energy that surrounds me.

121. I trust the timing of my spiritual journey.

122. My spirit is aligned with the energy of abundance and love.

123. I release fear and embrace the power of faith and trust.

124. My spiritual growth is a source of inspiration and clarity.

125. I honor the stillness that allows me to connect with my inner self.

126. My soul is at peace, and my heart is full of love.

127. I am open to the guidance of the universe.

128. My spiritual journey enriches every aspect of my life.

129. I release negativity and welcome healing and peace.

130. My spirit is resilient, and my soul is aligned with purpose.

131. I am grateful for the beauty of the spiritual path I'm on.

132. I trust the wisdom within me to guide my journey.

133. My soul is deeply connected to the energy of gratitude and love.

134. I honor the process of growth and transformation.

135. I release doubt and trust the flow of my spiritual journey.

136. My spiritual practice is a reflection of my inner strength.

137. I am open to the beauty of the present moment.

138. My soul is aligned with the energy of peace and purpose.

139. I am grateful for the clarity my spiritual practice brings.

140. My spiritual journey is a source of joy and inspiration.

141. I release fear and embrace the light of healing and love.

142. I trust the divine timing of my life and journey.

143. My spirit is aligned with the energy of abundance and peace.

144. I honor my connection to the divine within me.

145. I release negativity and welcome the light of healing.

146. My spiritual growth is a celebration of my resilience.

147. I am grounded in the present and open to its lessons.

148. My soul is nourished by the energy of love and peace.

149. I trust the process of spiritual alignment and growth.

150. My spiritual journey brings me closer to the life I desire.

REFLECTION PROMPT:

Take a moment to reflect on your spiritual journey. What areas of your life feel most aligned, and where do you feel growth is needed? Choose one affirmation to guide you as you nurture your inner peace and alignment.

Spiritual growth is a journey, not a destination. These affirmations are here to help you deepen your connection with your inner self, embrace peace, and live in alignment with your purpose. Let's continue on this transformative path.

CHAPTER 12:
AFFIRMATIONS FOR PATIENCE AND TRUST IN THE JOURNEY

"You don't make progress by standing on the sidelines, whimpering and complaining. You make progress by implementing ideas."
—Shirley Chisholm

Patience and trust are essential companions on life's journey. They remind us that growth and progress take time, and the road to fulfillment is often winding and unpredictable. Shirley Chisholm's words encourage action and forward movement, even when the results are not immediate. This is the essence of trusting the process—taking steps forward with faith that everything is unfolding as it should.

This chapter offers affirmations to help you embrace patience, let go of the need to control every detail and trust that your efforts will bear fruit. They will remind you to stay grounded in your journey, even when the destination feels distant.

150 Affirmations for Patience and Trust in the Journey

1. I trust that everything is unfolding in perfect timing.

2. Patience is a gift I give to myself and my journey.

3. I am confident that my efforts will lead to success.

4. I release the need to rush and allow life to flow naturally.

5. I trust the process, even when I cannot see the outcome.

6. I am grateful for the lessons that come with waiting.

7. My journey is unique, and I honor its pace.

8. I release frustration and embrace peace in the present moment.

9. I am patient with myself as I grow and evolve.

10. I trust that all good things will come to me in due time.

11. I embrace the waiting period as a time for reflection and growth.

12. I am at peace with where I am, knowing I am on the right path.

13. I release doubt and trust the unfolding of my life.

14. I am patient with others as they navigate their own journeys.

15. I trust that the universe has a plan for me.

16. I allow myself to move forward with ease and grace.

17. My patience brings me clarity and inner peace.

18. I release the need to control and trust in the process.

19. I am confident that my hard work will pay off in time.

20. I embrace uncertainty as a natural part of the journey.

21. I trust that the timing of my life is perfect, even when it feels slow.

22. I am grateful for the moments of stillness that foster growth.

23. I release worry and replace it with trust and patience.

24. My journey is a reflection of my inner strength and resilience.

25. I am patient with myself as I navigate new challenges.

26. I trust that every step I take is leading me toward my goals.

27. I release anxiety about the future and focus on the present.

28. I am open to unexpected detours that bring growth and learning.

29. My patience is a reflection of my inner peace and confidence.

30. I trust that I am exactly where I need to be at this moment.

31. I embrace the journey, even when it feels uncertain.

32. I release the need for immediate results and trust the process.

33. I am confident that my persistence will lead to success.

34. My patience allows me to appreciate each step of the journey.

35. I trust that the universe is working in my favor.

36. I release fear and replace it with faith in the process.

37. I am grateful for the small victories along the way.

38. I embrace each day as an opportunity to grow and learn.

39. My journey is unfolding perfectly, even when it feels slow.

40. I trust that the timing of my life is aligned with my purpose.

41. I release frustration and embrace patience as my guide.

42. My patience brings me closer to the life I desire.

43. I trust my ability to persevere through challenges.

44. I am open to the opportunities that come with waiting.

45. I release the need for control and allow life to unfold naturally.

46. I am confident in my ability to navigate the journey ahead.

47. My patience creates space for clarity and peace.

48. I trust that my dreams are manifesting in divine timing.

49. I release doubt and replace it with faith in the journey.

50. I am grateful for the progress I've made, no matter how small.

51. I trust that my efforts are bringing me closer to my goals.

52. I embrace the waiting period as a time for preparation.

53. My patience is a reflection of my trust in the universe.

54. I am at peace with the process of growth and transformation.

55. I trust that every delay is preparing me for something better.

56. I release the need to compare my journey to others.

57. My patience allows me to appreciate the beauty of the present.

58. I trust that the challenges I face are shaping me for greatness.

59. I am grateful for the time it takes to create meaningful change.

60. My journey is unique, and I honor its unfolding.

61. I release the need to rush and allow life to flow naturally.

62. I trust that everything I desire is on its way to me.

63. My patience is a testament to my resilience and faith.

64. I embrace the process of growth, no matter how long it takes.

65. I am confident that my efforts will bear fruit in time.

66. I trust the lessons that come with waiting and perseverance.

67. I release frustration and replace it with trust and peace.

68. My journey is a reflection of my strength and determination.

69. I am patient with myself as I work toward my goals.

70. I trust that the universe is guiding me toward my purpose.

71. My patience brings me closer to my dreams.

72. I release the need for instant gratification and embrace the process.

73. I am grateful for the progress I've made on my journey.

74. I trust that the timing of my life is perfect, even when it feels uncertain.

75. My patience allows me to enjoy each step of the journey.

76. I embrace the waiting period as a time for self-reflection.

77. I am confident that my persistence will lead to success.

78. I release worry and focus on the opportunities in front of me.

79. I trust that the universe is aligning everything in my favor.

80. My patience is a reflection of my inner peace and strength.

81. I am open to the growth that comes with time and experience.

82. I release the need to rush and allow myself to flow with ease.

83. My journey is unfolding perfectly, even when it feels slow.

84. I trust the process and embrace the lessons along the way.

85. I am confident that I am on the right path to my goals.

86. My patience allows me to see the beauty in each moment.

87. I release fear and replace it with trust and confidence.

88. I am grateful for the time it takes to create lasting change.

89. My patience is a reminder of my strength and resilience.

90. I trust that every delay is leading me toward something greater.

91. I embrace the process of growth and transformation.

92. My patience allows me to approach life with grace and ease.

93. I release frustration and replace it with faith in the journey.

94. I am confident that my dreams are manifesting in divine timing.

95. My patience allows me to savor each step of the journey.

96. I trust that the universe is aligning everything perfectly for me.

97. I release the need for control and allow life to unfold naturally.

98. My patience is a reflection of my trust in the process.

99. I am open to the lessons that come with waiting and perseverance.

100. I am confident in my ability to navigate the journey ahead.

101. I am grateful for the moments of stillness that prepare me for what's to come.

102. I trust that every experience is shaping me into the person I am meant to be.

103. I release impatience and embrace the natural flow of life.

104. My patience allows me to enjoy the beauty of the present moment.

105. I trust that the universe is working behind the scenes for my highest good.

106. I embrace the journey as much as the destination.

107. I release fear and step into faith with every breath I take.

108. I am open to the surprises that life has in store for me.

109. My patience helps me stay grounded and at peace.

110. I trust that my efforts are creating a solid foundation for the future.

111. I am grateful for the quiet moments that bring clarity and focus.

112. My patience reflects my belief in myself and my path.

113. I release the need to compare my timeline to anyone else's.

114. I am confident that my persistence will lead to the results I desire.

115. I trust that every small step I take will move me closer to my dreams.

116. My patience allows me to appreciate the lessons hidden in the journey

117. I release anxiety and choose to trust the process of life.

118. I am grateful for the opportunity to grow through waiting.

119. I trust the universe's plan for my life, even when I can't see it fully.

120. My patience strengthens my spirit and calms my mind.

121. I embrace the detours as part of my unique journey.

122. I release the need for perfection and embrace progress instead.

123. My patience brings clarity to my intentions and goals.

124. I trust that the challenges I face are helping me grow stronger.

125. I am grateful for the time it takes to create something meaningful.

126. My patience is an act of self-love and self-care.

127. I trust that the universe's timing is always better than my own.

128. I release frustration and replace it with faith in my journey.

129. My patience allows me to find joy in every step of the process.

130. I trust that my dreams are unfolding exactly as they should.

131. I am confident that my resilience will see me through any challenge.

132. My patience helps me stay focused and calm.

133. I release the need to rush and allow myself to enjoy the moment.

134. I trust that every delay is a blessing in disguise.

135. I am grateful for the opportunities to learn and grow through waiting.

136. My patience helps me see the beauty in the journey, not just the outcome.

137. I trust that the universe is guiding me toward my greatest good.

138. I release fear and embrace trust in the timing of my life.

139. My patience allows me to approach challenges with grace.

140. I am confident that my hard work will pay off in due time.

141. I trust that every step I take is part of a bigger plan.

142. My patience brings me peace and contentment in the present.

143. I release the need for instant results and focus on steady progress.

144. I am grateful for the clarity that patience brings to my life.

145. My journey is unique, and I honor every twist and turn.

146. I trust that the universe is aligning everything for my success.

147. My patience allows me to stay calm and centered in all situations.

148. I release doubt and replace it with unwavering confidence in my path.

149. I am open to the lessons and blessings that come with time.

150. My patience and trust in the journey are guiding me toward a fulfilling life.

REFLECTION PROMPT:

What area of your life requires patience and trust right now? Reflect on an affirmation from this chapter that resonates with you and repeat it daily to encourage calm and confidence as you move forward.

Patience is not passive—it's a powerful act of trust in your journey and your ability to persevere. These affirmations remind you that everything unfolds in its own time. Let's continue to embrace the beauty of the journey as we move forward to the next chapter.

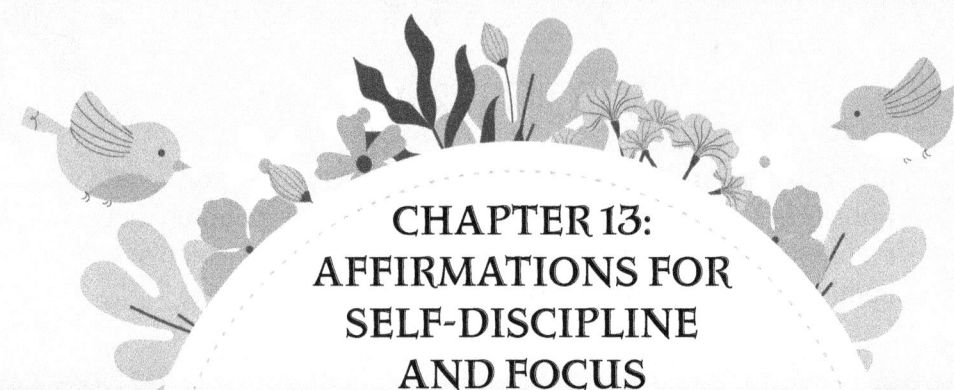

CHAPTER 13:
AFFIRMATIONS FOR
SELF-DISCIPLINE
AND FOCUS

"Don't let anyone rob you of your imagination, your creativity, or your curiosity. It's your place in the world; it's your life. Go on and do all you can with it, and make it the life you want to live."
—Mae Jemison

Self-discipline and focus are the keys to unlocking potential and achieving dreams. They empower you to set boundaries, remain consistent, and channel your energy toward meaningful goals. Mae Jemison's words encourage staying true to your vision, fueling the drive to build a life that reflects your unique aspirations and values.

This chapter offers affirmations designed to fortify your self-discipline, sharpen your focus, and inspire a steadfast commitment to your goals. These affirmations will remind you that with dedication and clarity, no goal is beyond your reach.

150 Affirmations for Self-Discipline and Focus

1. I am focused and committed to my goals.

2. My self-discipline strengthens with every choice I make.

3. I am in control of my thoughts, actions, and decisions.

4. I prioritize what truly matters to me.

5. My focus drives me to achieve great things.

6. I trust my ability to stay on track and reach my goals.

7. I release distractions and remain centered on my purpose.

8. I am disciplined in the pursuit of my dreams.

9. My determination fuels my success.

10. I have the power to say no to what does not serve me.

11. My focus is unwavering, even in challenging times.

12. I am consistent in my efforts to create the life I desire.

13. I release procrastination and embrace action.

14. My self-discipline leads me to extraordinary results.

15. I am proud of my ability to remain committed to my goals.

16. I trust my ability to overcome distractions and stay focused.

17. My discipline is a reflection of my love for myself.

18. I am clear about what I want and take steps to achieve it.

19. I prioritize my goals and let go of unnecessary distractions.

20. My self-discipline is the foundation of my success.

21. I am confident in my ability to make intentional choices.

22. I focus on what matters and release what does not.

23. My determination is stronger than any obstacle.

24. I am consistent in the small actions that lead to big results.

25. I trust my ability to stay committed, even when it's challenging.

26. My focus allows me to make steady progress every day.

27. I am disciplined in creating healthy habits that support my goals.

28. I embrace consistency as the key to achieving my dreams.

29. I am proud of my ability to stay focused and productive.

30. My self-discipline strengthens with every action I take.

31. I trust my ability to manage my time wisely.

32. I release distractions and prioritize what truly matters.

33. My focus is my superpower, and I use it wisely.

34. I am committed to my growth and success.

35. My self-discipline helps me stay aligned with my goals.

36. I make decisions that reflect my long-term vision.

37. My focus allows me to accomplish more with less effort.

38. I trust my ability to remain consistent and dedicated.

39. I release excuses and embrace responsibility for my actions.

40. I am disciplined in creating routines that support my goals.

41. My focus empowers me to stay on track, no matter what.

42. I am proud of my ability to remain determined and disciplined.

43. I trust that my hard work will lead to meaningful results.

44. My self-discipline creates space for growth and achievement.

45. I am committed to staying focused on what truly matters to me.

46. I release the need for perfection and focus on progress.

47. My discipline inspires others to stay committed to their goals.

48. I am capable of overcoming distractions with ease.

49. My focus allows me to make meaningful progress every day.

50. I am disciplined in managing my time and energy.

51. I trust my ability to remain consistent in my efforts.

52. My self-discipline is a powerful tool for creating change.

53. I prioritize my goals over short-term distractions.

54. I release procrastination and take action toward my dreams.

55. My focus is my greatest asset in achieving success.

56. I am proud of the consistency I bring to my work and life.

57. I trust my ability to stay disciplined, even when it's difficult.

58. My self-discipline helps me achieve my greatest potential.

59. I am clear about my priorities and act on them daily.

60. My focus allows me to achieve my goals efficiently and effectively.

61. I am disciplined in following through on my commitments.

62. I trust my ability to remain focused in any situation.

63. My self-discipline is a reflection of my dedication to my dreams.

64. I prioritize my long-term vision over short-term distractions.

65. I release fear and embrace action as the path to success.

66. My focus empowers me to create the life I envision.

67. I am proud of my ability to remain consistent and committed.

68. I trust that my self-discipline will lead to extraordinary results.

69. My self-discipline is a daily practice that strengthens my resolve.

70. I prioritize my goals and release distractions with ease.

71. My focus allows me to accomplish what I set out to do.

72. I am committed to staying disciplined in all areas of my life.

73. My self-discipline inspires me to take meaningful action daily.

74. I release excuses and take responsibility for my progress.

75. My focus is unwavering, even when challenges arise.

76. I trust my ability to remain consistent, no matter the circumstances.

77. My self-discipline helps me create a life of purpose and meaning.

78. I prioritize what matters most and let go of the rest.

79. My focus allows me to make steady progress toward my goals.

80. I am proud of my ability to stay determined and disciplined.

81. I trust my ability to overcome distractions and stay on track.

82. My self-discipline is my greatest strength in achieving success.

83. I release doubt and embrace confidence in my discipline.

84. My focus empowers me to achieve extraordinary results.

85. I am committed to showing up for myself every day.

86. My self-discipline allows me to live in alignment with my values.

87. I prioritize my goals and remain consistent in my actions.

88. I trust my ability to stay disciplined, even when it's hard.

89. My focus helps me achieve clarity and purpose in my life.

90. I am proud of the self-discipline I bring to my journey.

91. I release distractions and remain centered on my purpose.

92. My self-discipline is a reflection of my inner strength and resolve.

93. I prioritize what truly matters and release what does not.

94. My focus allows me to achieve my goals with precision and intention.

95. I trust that my hard work will lead to meaningful results.

96. My self-discipline helps me create positive habits and routines.

97. I release excuses and embrace responsibility for my choices.

98. My focus empowers me to take meaningful steps toward my goals.

99. I am proud of the determination I bring to every aspect of my life.

100. My self-discipline strengthens my confidence and self-respect.

101. I am capable of staying disciplined, even in the face of challenges.

102. My focus allows me to remain clear and intentional in my actions.

103. I prioritize my vision and let go of distractions.

104. My self-discipline helps me stay aligned with my highest purpose.

105. I trust my ability to remain consistent and committed.

106. I am proud of the progress I make through disciplined effort.

107. My focus empowers me to achieve the life I envision.

108. My self-discipline inspires me to keep moving forward.

109. I release self-doubt and embrace the power of action.

110. My focus allows me to stay on track and achieve my goals.

111. I am confident in my ability to remain disciplined and determined.

112. My self-discipline leads me to a life of fulfillment and success.

113. I prioritize my goals and release the rest with ease.

114. My focus helps me create the life I desire.

115. I trust my ability to remain consistent and focused.

116. My self-discipline is a reflection of my love for myself.

117. I am proud of the determination I bring to my dreams.

118. My focus empowers me to achieve extraordinary outcomes.

119. I release fear and embrace confidence in my abilities.

120. My self-discipline allows me to live with intention and purpose.

121. I am capable of staying focused, no matter the distractions.

122. My focus strengthens my resolve to achieve my goals.

123. My self-discipline helps me create a meaningful and fulfilling life.

124. I trust my ability to overcome obstacles with determination.

125. I am proud of the focus I bring to every step of my journey.

126. My self-discipline allows me to remain clear and intentional.

127. My focus drives me to achieve success with clarity and purpose.

128. I prioritize my goals and remain consistent in my actions.

129. My self-discipline is my foundation for achieving greatness.

130. I release doubt and trust in my ability to stay disciplined.

131. My focus helps me stay aligned with my vision for the future.

132. My self-discipline inspires me to take bold and intentional action.

133. I am confident in my ability to achieve anything I set my mind to.

134. My focus empowers me to create meaningful change in my life.

135. My self-discipline allows me to live with integrity and intention.

136. I prioritize my dreams and release distractions with ease.

137. My focus strengthens my determination to succeed.

138. My self-discipline is a reflection of my inner strength and resilience.

139. I trust my ability to stay committed, no matter the challenges.

140. My focus empowers me to remain clear and intentional in my goals.

141. My self-discipline helps me create positive habits and routines.

142. I release procrastination and embrace consistent effort.

143. My focus allows me to achieve my goals with clarity and intention.

144. I trust my ability to stay disciplined, even in uncertain times.

145. My self-discipline inspires me to create a life of purpose and joy.

146. I prioritize what matters most and release the rest.

147. My focus drives me to achieve extraordinary results.

148. My self-discipline strengthens my confidence and self-respect.

149. I am proud of the determination I bring to my journey.

150. My focus allows me to create the life I've always envisioned.

REFLECTION PROMPT:

Think about an area in your life where self-discipline or focus is needed. Which affirmation resonates most with this area? Write it down and repeat it daily to help anchor your actions to your goals.

Self-discipline and focus are the cornerstones of growth and success. These affirmations are here to remind you of your strength, determination, and capacity to create meaningful progress. Let's continue building on this momentum in the next chapter.

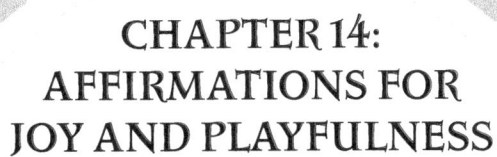

CHAPTER 14:
AFFIRMATIONS FOR
JOY AND PLAYFULNESS

"If you're always trying to be normal, you will never know how amazing you can be."
—Maya Angelou

Joy and playfulness are not just about having fun—they are essential components of a fulfilling life. They remind us to take a break from the weight of responsibilities and embrace the beauty of the present moment. Maya Angelou's words encourage stepping outside the norm and allowing yourself to experience the freedom and creativity that come with being unapologetically you.

This chapter is about cultivating joy, rediscovering the magic of play, and bringing lighthearted energy into your life. These affirmations will inspire you to let go of stress, invite laughter, and create moments that bring you pure happiness.

150 Affirmations for Joy and Playfulness

1. I embrace the joy that is always present in my life.

2. I allow myself to laugh freely and often.

3. My days are filled with moments of lighthearted happiness.

4. I am open to the magic of spontaneity and fun.

5. I choose to see life as an adventure full of possibilities.

6. My playful energy inspires creativity and excitement.

7. I release stress and welcome joy into my heart.

8. I am worthy of moments of pure, unfiltered happiness.

9. I embrace my inner child and celebrate life's simple pleasures.

10. My joy is a reflection of my love for myself and life.

11. I am open to discovering new ways to experience happiness.

12. I permit myself to let go and have fun.

13. I create space in my life for laughter and play.

14. My happiness radiates and inspires those around me.

15. I am free to explore the world with curiosity and wonder.

16. I choose to focus on the good and let go of the rest.

17. I allow myself to enjoy life without guilt or worry.

18. I celebrate the small joys that make life beautiful.

19. My heart is open to the abundance of happiness around me.

20. I embrace playfulness as a way to nurture my spirit.

21. I am grateful for the moments of joy that brighten my day.

22. I trust that joy is always available to me.

23. I let go of fear and embrace the freedom of being myself.

24. I am open to unexpected moments of happiness.

25. My playful spirit brings balance and energy to my life.

26. I choose to see the humor in life's challenges.

27. I create memories that bring me lasting happiness.

28. I am deserving of a life filled with laughter and joy.

29. I am grateful for the people and experiences that make me smile.

30. I release negativity and replace it with gratitude for the good.

31. My happiness is a priority, and I honor it daily.

32. I allow myself to be silly and carefree when the moment calls.

33. I find joy in the little things that brighten my day.

34. My heart is light, and my spirit is free.

35. I embrace the joy that comes from living authentically.

36. I trust that happiness flows naturally into my life.

37. I celebrate the beauty and wonder of the world around me.

38. I am open to creating moments of happiness wherever I go.

39. My laughter is healing and uplifting for myself and others.

40. I let go of perfection and embrace the joy of imperfection.

41. I choose to fill my life with positivity and fun.

42. I am grateful for the ability to experience joy in all its forms.

43. I celebrate life's surprises with excitement and gratitude.

44. My playfulness is a source of strength and inspiration.

45. I am worthy of the happiness I seek and create.

46. I trust that joy is a natural part of my life.

47. I release stress and embrace the lightness of being.

48. I create opportunities to experience joy every day.

49. My happiness is contagious and brings light to others.

50. I am free to express myself with creativity and humor.

51. I am open to the laughter that comes from life's unexpected moments.

52. I celebrate the unique ways I find joy and fulfillment.

53. My playful energy brings balance to my busy life.

54. I let go of worry and replace it with hope and positivity.

55. I choose to see the beauty in every moment.

56. I am grateful for the happiness that fills my life.

57. I allow myself to pause and enjoy life's playful moments.

58. I embrace the joy of trying new things and taking risks.

59. My spirit is playful, curious, and full of wonder.

60. I trust that happiness is always within my reach.

61. I celebrate the laughter that connects me to others.

62. I choose to focus on what brings me joy and peace.

63. My heart is open to the possibilities of happiness around me.

64. I am grateful for the opportunities to create joyful memories.

65. I release stress and invite more playfulness into my day.

66. I am deserving of happiness in every aspect of my life.

67. My playful energy helps me stay young at heart.

68. I trust that life is full of moments to celebrate and enjoy.

69. I embrace the freedom that comes with laughter and joy.

70. I create a life that reflects my playful and adventurous spirit.

71. I am grateful for the ability to bring joy to others.

72. My happiness is a reflection of my inner peace and balance.

73. I let go of limitations and embrace the fun of exploration.

74. I choose to approach life with a sense of humor and lightness.

75. I am free to find joy in unexpected places.

76. My playful energy opens doors to new opportunities.

77. I celebrate the moments that bring me laughter and peace.

78. I allow myself to feel joy without hesitation.

79. My happiness is a reflection of my gratitude for life.

80. I embrace the present moment as a source of joy and inspiration.

81. I trust that happiness will always find its way to me.

82. I create a life filled with love, laughter, and adventure.

83. My playful spirit is a reminder to enjoy the journey.

84. I am grateful for the beauty and magic of life.

85. I let go of worry and choose to focus on joy instead.

86. I trust that my playful energy will attract positivity and peace.

87. I celebrate my ability to find joy in the simplest things.

88. I create space for happiness to grow and thrive in my life.

89. I am worthy of the joy and laughter that life offers.

90. My happiness is a gift I give to myself and others.

91. I release stress and invite laughter into my day.

92. I am open to the magic and wonder of every moment.

93. My playful energy helps me navigate life with ease and grace.

94. I trust that joy is always within my reach.

95. I am grateful for the happiness that brightens my life.

96. I celebrate the freedom to live with playfulness and creativity.

97. I choose to focus on what makes me smile and laugh.

98. My heart is full of gratitude for life's joyful surprises.

99. I embrace the power of playfulness to heal and inspire.

100. I am open to the happiness that life has to offer.

101. I celebrate the light-hearted moments that bring me joy.

102. My playful energy connects me to my inner child.

103. I trust that life's challenges are balanced with moments of joy.

104. I choose to see the humor in life's ups and downs.

105. I am grateful for the gift of laughter that brightens my days.

106. My happiness is rooted in the love I have for myself and others.

107. I release negativity and replace it with playfulness and hope.

108. I am proud of my ability to create joy wherever I go.

109. My playful energy inspires those around me to embrace fun.

110. I celebrate the beauty of living in the moment.

111. I choose to let go of what weighs me down and embrace joy.

112. I trust that laughter is a powerful tool for healing and connection.

113. I am open to the happiness that comes with being present.

114. My playful spirit reminds me to celebrate life every day.

115. I create a life filled with laughter, love, and adventure.

116. I am grateful for the joy that flows through my life.

117. I let go of stress and replace it with laughter and peace.

118. My playful energy helps me see life through fresh eyes.

119. I trust that joy is always within my grasp.

120. I am deserving of the happiness I create and share.

121. I embrace the moments of fun that bring balance to my life.

122. I celebrate the freedom to be myself unapologetically.

123. My playful energy helps me navigate challenges with optimism.

124. I trust that happiness is my natural state of being.

125. I am grateful for the opportunities to create joyful memories.

126. My laughter is a reflection of my gratitude for life.

127. I choose to approach each day with excitement and curiosity.

128. My playful spirit is a source of strength and resilience.

129. I celebrate the joy that comes from living authentically.

130. I trust that happiness is always available to me.

131. I am proud of my ability to find joy in the small things.

132. I release negativity and embrace the magic of play.

133. My playful energy allows me to connect deeply with others.

134. I create space for happiness to thrive in my life.

135. My joy is a reflection of my gratitude for the present moment.

136. I trust that laughter will always find its way to me.

137. I embrace the beauty and wonder of the world around me.

138. My playful energy inspires me to live boldly and fully.

139. I celebrate the happiness that comes from being true to myself.

140. I am open to the joy that life has to offer me.

141. My laughter is a reminder to enjoy the journey.

142. I choose to focus on the good and let go of the rest.

143. My playful energy helps me approach life with lightness and love.

144. I am grateful for the joy that fills my heart.

145. My happiness is a reflection of the love I have for myself.

146. I trust that joy is always within reach, no matter the circumstance.

147. I celebrate the freedom to live a life full of fun and laughter.

148. My playful energy helps me see life's beauty and potential.

149. I choose to let go of stress and embrace joy.

150. I am proud of my ability to create and sustain happiness in my life.

REFLECTION PROMPT:

What is one playful activity or joyful moment you can incorporate into your day today? Choose an affirmation from this chapter to guide you as you embrace the lightness of being.

Joy and playfulness are essential to living a balanced, fulfilling life. Let these affirmations remind you to take a breath, laugh freely, and celebrate the beauty of simply being. Let's continue our journey together in the next chapter.

PART 3:

INTEGRATION AND BEYOND

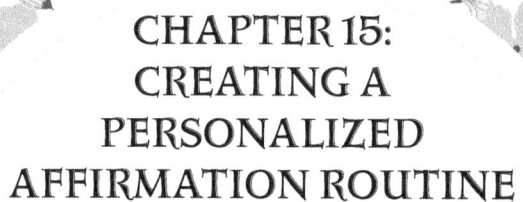

CHAPTER 15:
CREATING A
PERSONALIZED
AFFIRMATION ROUTINE

"First forget inspiration. Habit is more dependable. Habit will sustain you whether you're inspired or not. Habit will help you finish and polish your stories. Inspiration won't. Habit is persistence in practice."
—Octavia E. Butler

Affirmations are most powerful when practiced regularly and with intention. Like any tool, their impact depends on how and when you use them. A personalized routine can make affirmations an integral part of your daily life, grounding your thoughts, aligning your actions, and empowering you to stay focused on your goals.

This chapter is about helping you create a sustainable affirmation practice that fits seamlessly into your lifestyle. Whether you're a morning person, thrive in the quiet of the evening, or find time during busy moments, these steps will guide you in building a routine that works for you.

How to Create Your Affirmation Routine

1. Start with Purpose
- Reflect on why affirmations matter to you. Are you focusing on self-love, building resilience, or achieving a specific goal?
- Choose affirmations that align with your intentions and feel authentic.

Example: If your goal is to build confidence, select affirmations like "I am worthy of success" or "I trust my abilities."

2. Choose Your Timing
- **Morning:** Affirmations can set a positive tone for the day ahead. Pair them with your morning coffee or meditation.
- **Evening:** Use affirmations before bed to reflect on your progress and plant seeds for the next day.
- **Anytime:** Sneak affirmations into your daily routine.

Tip: Start small with 5-10 minutes a day and gradually increase the time as it becomes a habit.

3. Create a Ritual
- Tie your affirmations to an existing habit, such as brushing your teeth, journaling, or drinking tea.
- Repeat them out loud, write them down, or visualize them as already true.
- Experiment with different methods to discover what resonates most with you.

4. Build a Safe Space
- Choose a quiet, comfortable spot where you can focus without interruptions.
- Enhance your environment with calming elements like candles, plants, or soothing music.

5. Track Your Progress
- Keep a journal to reflect on how your affirmations are influencing your thoughts and actions.
- Write about shifts in your mindset, emotions, or behaviors.

Prompt: How do you feel after repeating affirmations? What changes have you noticed in your outlook?

6. Stay Flexible
- Life changes, and so do your goals and challenges. Update your affirmations to reflect your current needs and aspirations.
- Be kind to yourself if you miss a day. Consistency is important, but flexibility is key to sustaining your practice.

Sample Affirmation Routine

Here's an example to inspire your own routine:

Morning (5 minutes)
- Sit in a quiet space with your favorite drink.
- Repeat 5 affirmations aloud: "I am confident, I am strong, I am enough, I trust my intuition, I embrace the day with positivity."

Afternoon (3 minutes)
- Take a break at work or during errands.
- Reflect on 2 affirmations silently: "I am focused on my goals" and "I attract positive opportunities."

Evening (10 minutes)
- Write 3 affirmations in your journal: "I am grateful for today's lessons," "I trust in the timing of my life," and "I am proud of my progress."

Reflection Prompt:

What time of day feels most natural for practicing affirmations? Write down one affirmation that resonates with your current goals and experiment with incorporating it into your daily routine.

Creating a personalized affirmation routine is a powerful way to nurture your growth and align with your goals. By building consistency and intention into your practice, you'll create a foundation for lasting transformation. As we close this book, let's reflect on the transformation you've created and look forward to the opportunities ahead.

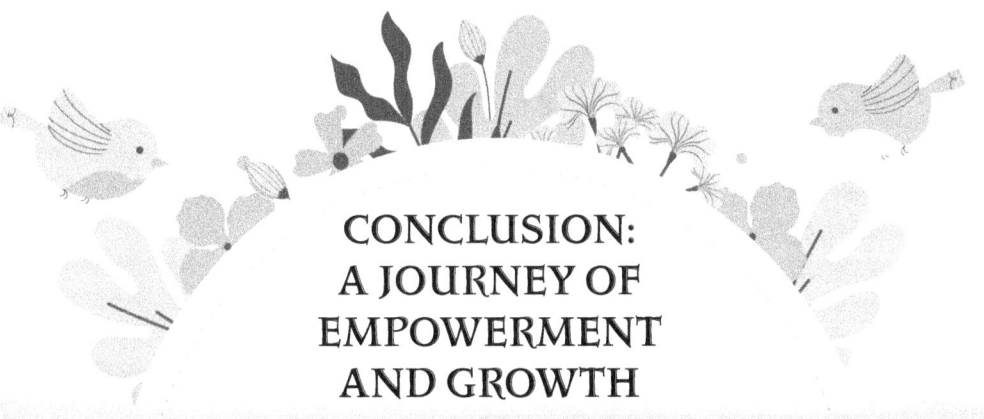

CONCLUSION:
A JOURNEY OF
EMPOWERMENT
AND GROWTH

"I am deliberate and afraid of nothing."
—Audre Lorde

Congratulations on taking this journey of self-discovery, empowerment, and growth. By embracing the power of affirmations, you've not only nurtured your mindset but also unlocked the potential to transform your life. Audre Lorde's words remind us of the strength and intention that come from claiming our power and walking confidently toward our dreams.

This book is more than just a collection of affirmations—it's a guide to helping you reclaim your voice, celebrate your individuality, and recognize the incredible light you bring into the world. Each affirmation you've spoken, written, or reflected upon has planted seeds of positivity, resilience, and joy. These seeds will continue to grow, shaping your thoughts, actions, and the life you create.

Reflecting on the Journey

As you turn the final page, take a moment to reflect on how far you've come:

- What affirmations resonated with you most deeply?
- How has your perspective shifted since beginning this practice?
- What changes have you noticed in your thoughts, relationships, or daily habits?

Every step you've taken is a testament to your courage, your commitment to growth, and your belief in a brighter, more empowered future.

Carrying Affirmations Forward

Affirmations are tools you can carry with you, no matter where life leads. Whether you're stepping into new opportunities, navigating challenges, or savoring moments of joy, affirmations will remain your steady companions. They remind you of your worth, your strength, and your ability to create the life you desire.

A Word of Encouragement

Remember, this is just the beginning. Growth is an ongoing journey, and affirmations are here to support you every step of the way. Some days will feel easier than others, and that's okay. Be patient with yourself, celebrate your progress, and trust in your ability to continue moving forward. You are worthy of love, success, joy, and fulfillment. You are powerful beyond measure. And you are capable of creating a life that reflects the incredible person you are.

Reflection Prompt:

What is one affirmation from this book that you want to carry with you every day? Write it down, make it visible, and let it guide you as you continue your journey.

Closing Inspiration

As you step forward, remember this: your words have power, your thoughts shape your reality, and your actions create change. Trust in yourself, believe in your dreams, and know that you are already enough.

You are deliberate. You are unafraid. And the best is yet to come.

Thank you for letting this book be a part of your journey. May it continue to inspire and empower you in ways both big and small.

With love and light.